A Visitor's Guide to Shakespeare's London

A Visitor's Guide to Shakespeare's London

David Thomas

PEN & SWORD
HISTORY

First published in Great Britain in 2016 by
Pen & Sword History
an imprint of
Pen & Sword Books Ltd
47 Church Street
Barnsley
South Yorkshire
S70 2AS

ISBN 978 1 47382 554 3

Typeset in Ehrhardt by
Mac Style Ltd, Bridlington, East Yorkshire
Printed and bound in the UK by CPI Group (UK) Ltd,
Croydon, CRO 4YY

Pen & Sword Books Ltd incorporates the imprints of Pen & Sword
Archaeology, Atlas, Aviation, Battleground, Discovery, Family
History, History, Maritime, Military, Naval, Politics, Railways,
Select, Transport, True Crime, and Fiction, Frontline Books, Leo
Cooper, Praetorian Press, Seaforth Publishing and Wharncliffe.

For a complete list of Pen & Sword titles please contact
PEN & SWORD BOOKS LIMITED
47 Church Street, Barnsley, South Yorkshire, S70 2AS, England
E-mail: enquiries@pen-and-sword.co.uk
Website: www.pen-and-sword.co.uk

Contents

Acknowledgements

I would like to thank Andrea Thomas for writing the sections on the walks and on buildings that Shakespeare might have seen and also for her photography. Thanks also to Michael Braund for producing the map of London in Shakespeare's time. Michael must be the speediest cartographer in the world – and amazingly helpful.

Introduction

In many ways, the London of Shakespeare's day was surprisingly like our own – it had inns and taverns, sports and the theatre. Shopping, gambling and drinking were as popular then as they are now. People probably smoked more than they do now, although even King James warned of the injurious effects of tobacco. For the better off, sugar was as big a part of their diet as it is for the poor in the twenty-first century, although our dentists are better at dealing with its effects. Just as today you can see City businessmen discussing important issues in London's many coffee shops, so you would have seen them gathering at New Change to hear the latest gossip and buy and sell. The traffic in London was probably worse than it is now – a city designed for people to walk in had become overwhelmed by carts and carriages.

The difference between the Londoners and the country dwellers was becoming increasingly apparent. People in the country saw Londoners as soft and not living the authentic life. They called them 'Bow-Bell Cockneys' and eaters of buttered toast. But at the same time, they loved to read about the dangers of visiting the City. Thomas Dekker and his fellow writers played along with this fear by writing a series of books describing the tricks that would be played on the unsuspecting country man or woman who dared visit the great metropolis.

But if you look at Tudor London as something like a modern city, you will suddenly be brought up short by realising that it was also a medieval city – the water supply was, frankly, unreliable. The City was frequently overwhelmed by outbreaks of the plague and other diseases were rife. The citizens enjoyed barbaric sports such as bear baiting and cock fighting and if time hung heavily on their hands, they could go and enjoy a nice execution – hanging, burning or beheading, take your pick. It was also a world where status and your position in the hierarchy mattered very much.

Physically much of the London that Shakespeare knew has been destroyed by the Great Fire, redevelopment over several centuries and the Blitz, but there is enough to get glimpses of what he would have seen. Despite the efforts of the Victorians, much of London's street plan survives and a surprisingly large number of buildings remain that Shakespeare would have been familiar with.

London exists because of and is defined by its river. However, the river Shakespeare knew is quite different from the modern one we see. It was much wider, since the embankments had not been built, and it had fewer bridges – London Bridge was the only bridge between the estuary and Kingston. The river was also much busier, bringing food and supplies to the City and carrying thousands of passengers a day up to Windsor or down to Greenwich and Gravesend or simply from Whitehall to the theatres on the south bank. Sadly, one of the great features of Shakespeare's river – the large flock of swans that gathered there – has long gone.

In many ways it was safer than the modern city. There was a moderately effective police force in the form of the Watch and the streets were lit at night. There were a lot more cheats and tricksters on the streets, but these days they have moved to the Internet. Above all, there was no political crime or terror. Queen Elizabeth could enjoy herself on the frozen Thames in company with thousands of her subjects, while King James could attend a cockfight in a pub yard. Neither of these activities would be conceivable today without a heavy police presence and probably a stage-managed audience.

It was, increasingly, a city that welcomed and profited from tourism. By the reign of James I a London season was developing. The better off sort would come up to London in the autumn to enjoy the theatre and the inns, sightseeing and visiting the royal palaces and the historic towns which were a half-day's ride or a boat trip away. There were other pleasures too – a zoo at the Tower of London, a chance to climb the tower of St Paul's Cathedral or visiting the bookshops in the surrounding streets, or perhaps a boat trip to Greenwich to see the hulk of Sir Francis Drake's *Golden*

Hind. If they wanted, visitors could dress up in dandified clothes and swagger about in Paul's Walk or another fashionable rendezvous. The visitors would stay in town until the spring when they would go home to enjoy the pleasures of the summer but would return next autumn, glad to get away from the tedium of country life. There were other gentry, often younger sons or unmarried older women, who moved to London because it was cheaper – it was possible to live in a smaller house or rent rooms and to dispense with most servants.

As a result of this annual influx of visitors, the necessary infrastructure for tourism began to develop. There were inns and taverns to provide accommodation as well as restaurants. It was possible to hire a carriage and driver if you wanted to visit the country or to ride post horses from one inn to the next. There was lots for tourists to do and see, but the Londoners had already cottoned on to the idea of tipping – foreign visitors often complained about the necessity to tip virtually everybody.

As London became popular with British tourists, it also began to attract visitors from overseas and facilities were developed for them. There were Italian and French inn-keepers and provision was made for them to worship in their own churches – Protestant or Catholic.

We will be making this visit to Shakespeare's London in the company of some of the overseas visitors who came and recorded what they had observed. The first visitor we will meet is Alessandro Magno, a Venetian who came in 1562. Next is L. Grenade, who was probably Luis de Granada and a member of a family of horsemen, merchants, royal servants and diplomats who lived in London, the Low Countries and France; he wrote an account of London in 1578. Paul Hentzner, a German lawyer born in 1558, was a tutor to a young nobleman and spent the period 1596–9 travelling with him through Switzerland, France, England and Italy and published his account of his travels in 1616. Then there is Thomas Platter, a highly self-opinionated Swiss medical student who came in 1599, and Horatio Busino, the chaplain to the Venetian Ambassador, who arrived in 1617.

We will also be listening to three local boys – first, the incomparable John Stow whose magnificent *Survey of London* is the start of all explorations of the capital in the late sixteenth century. Then there is Fynes Moryson, son of a Lincolnshire gentleman who spent the 1590s exploring Europe and the Near East, including England. Naturally, he could not refrain from commenting on the superiority of some aspects of English life. Finally, Thomas Dekker, entertaining pamphleteer and moderately successful playwright who achieved unlikely posthumous success when his poem 'Golden Slumbers' was adapted by The Beatles. A man of trenchant views on almost everything, he is always worth listening to.

So we have our guides, let us start exploring.

Chapter One

Getting Your Bearings

L ondon is a large city with a population of about 200,000. It is smaller than Constantinople, Paris or Naples but larger than Venice, Seville or Lisbon. It is a great destination for a tourist, offering amazing opportunities for shopping, visiting the theatre, looking at historical sights and for escape to the countryside. Like most cities, there are problems with crime and disease, but most tourists who come here have an excellent time.

When to Visit London

The most obvious season might appear to be the summer when the weather is warmer, the difficulties of travel over land or across the Channel are less and there are more opportunities for entertainment. Life in Tudor and Stuart England is largely lived outdoors and so it would make sense to visit at a time when it is easier to be outside.

However, consider the alternative. Coming to London in the winter is much healthier, particularly because the plague normally occurs in the summer after a warm spring.

London is much busier in the winter and hence there is more entertainment and more to do. The City is at its busiest during the period when the main law courts in Westminster are open for business. This begins on 6 October and continues until 8 July, at which point the judges, lawyers and litigants pack up their documents and bags and set off to their homes in the country where they occupy themselves with such important matters as the harvest, leaving London quiet and empty.

As well as those concerned with the law, London also has another floating population, of gentlemen who come up to town for the season.

This begins in the autumn, reaches its climax at Christmas and is over by June. There are many reasons for a gentleman to come to London – to attend Parliament, to buy land (London is the centre of the land market) or to borrow money (London is the centre of the money market and the London merchants are the great lenders). Some may even be looking to find a wife. Daughters and widows of wealthy City merchants are always an attractive prospect.

The main reason for coming to London, however, is that it offers far more pleasures than a dull life in the country. In 1605, John Wynn of Gwydir wrote, 'I am resolved to spend the greatest part of the rest of my lyf for the winter and spring quarter abowt London'. Wynn lived in one of the most rural areas of North Wales, and like many other gentry he had experienced the pleasures of London during the two years he spent at the Inns of Court learning the law. Some members of wealthier families, particularly younger sons and widows have moved to London because it is possible to live more cheaply there than in the country. King James dislikes this influx of gentlemen to the capital, feeling that they are neglecting their duties in the country and failing to support the local economy by spending money in their own towns and villages. The king has tried to prevent them from coming but he might as well stand against a waterfall.

The gentlemen who do come to London are famous for their ostentatious way of dressing. As Ben Jonson said, 'First to be an accomplished gentleman – that is a gentleman of the time – you must give over housekeeping in the country and live together in the City among gallants where, at your first appearance, twere good you turned four or five acres of your best land into two or three trunks of apparel.'

The money that visitors from the country spend in London means that the London merchants, particularly the sellers of luxury goods, have grown prosperous and there have been a number of new shopping developments as a result. The growth of the London Season means that there are plenty of places to stay and to eat and also many entertainments. Thomas Platter said, 'I have never seen more taverns and ale-houses in my whole life than in London.'

The best entertainments are to be had in the winter months. These start with the Lord Mayor's Day on 29 October. There are also celebrations over the Christmas period; the fleet bringing the new wine from Bordeaux arrives in December and there are theatrical performances and feasting leading up to twelfth night on 5 January. If you do come in the winter and are very lucky, the Thames will be frozen over and there will be a frost fair on the river ice.

How to Get There

For those coming from overseas, there are a number of options. You can get a boat from Calais to Dover or from Calais to Gravesend. The Gravesend voyage is very difficult and its length depends on the weather and the tidal conditions on the Thames: boats need to wait to catch the incoming tide. It took Horatio Busino 23 hours to travel on this route in 1617. He spent his time observing his fellow passengers: 'musicians, women, merchants, bearded Jews, tatterdemalions and gentlemen crowded together'. From Gravesend you can get a coach to London, or take a ferry up the river. If you catch the ferry after breakfast, and the tide is in your favour, you should be in London by 2pm. There are two sorts of ferry on this route – the common ferry run by Gravesend Council, which costs 2d., and the faster and more exclusive tilt boats, which cost 4d.

For those travelling via Dover, the most popular option is to go by road to Gravesend and then by ferry to London. If you are fit enough to ride then it is possible to hire post horses from an inn. The horse will take you between 10 and 20 miles to another inn where you drop it off and hire another one for the next stage. This will cost you 3d. per mile plus 6d. to the post boy who will return the horse to its original inn. In 1599, Thomas Platter did the reverse journey from Gravesend to Dover – 44 miles in 5 hours, but found it very uncomfortable as he was not used to the small English saddles. People with more money or who cannot face a long ride can hire a coach or a two-wheeled waggon, which is the way Platter travelled up from Dover. The cost of a four-wheeled coach is about 16s. a day plus food for the horses and coachman. Unfortunately, the roads are in very poor condition. In theory people are required to provide their labour and carts to help maintain the king's highways, but many do not do so or pay a small fine to get out of the work.

London's Population

London's population has been growing rapidly, mostly because of migration from the rest of England, Wales and Scotland – some gentry, but mostly poorer people looking for work. The majority of Londoners are first-generation immigrants. The population of London is very young – about a quarter of those moving to London are aged between 11 and 20 and the number of apprentices has doubled from about 7,000 in 1550 to about 15,000 in 1600. There is a great deal of poverty. Probably 30,000 people are poor, old, unemployed, beggars, vagrants or rely on very short-term jobs to get by.

People born in London are increasingly coming to be referred to as cockneys. The original meaning of this word (which is referred to by Chaucer) is an offensive term used by countrymen to describe pampered or soft people who live in towns, unlike the stout British yeomen who dwell in the country. It is more and more being used to mean people who were born within the sound of the bells of St Mary-le-Bow. Samuel Rowlands in his book of satires, *Letting of Humour's Blood in the Head Vaine*, published in 1600, talked about a 'Bow-Bell Cockney'. In 1617, Fynes Moryson said, 'Londiners and all within the sound of Bow-bell, are in reproach called Cocknies and eaters of buttered tostes'.

There is a stable population of about 7,000 people from overseas. Most have come because of religious persecution in their home countries – France and the Netherlands. They tend to live in Southwark and the parish of St Katherine-by-the-Tower. The number of immigrants is declining with increased religious toleration in France. The attitude of Londoners to foreigners is hard to gauge – some visitors believe that they are very hostile; in 1588, the Florentine writer Petruccio Ubaldini said it was easier 'to find flocks of white crows than one Englishman who loves a foreigner'. In 1592, Jacob Rathgeb said Londoners were 'extremely proud and overbearing … they care little for foreigners but laugh and scoff at them'. On the other hand, Thomas Platter said that 'since the wars in the Netherlands and France [the population of London] has increased by many thousands of families who have settled in this city for religion's sake and these have been very kindly received, and special places of worship allotted to them'. One issue is dress: Horatio Busino, who visited in 1617, said, 'Foreigners are ill regarded, not to say detested in London, so sensible people dress in the English fashion or in that of France which is adopted by nearly all the court.'

Getting Orientated

London stretches about 3 miles from Wapping in the east to Westminster in the west and about 2 miles north to south (including Southwark across the river). Visitors are sometimes puzzled that London does not have a centre. This is because it is really three separate areas: the City of London, Westminster and Southwark. The City of London is the old, walled city and is the centre for trade and commerce. Westminster is the area of the royal palace of Whitehall, the law courts, Parliament and is, increasingly, where the aristocrats live. Southwark lies south of the river and is the place for things that are not quite respectable enough for the City of London and certainly not respectable enough for Westminster.

One way to get to understand London is to hire a horse, or even walk to Highgate which is a small country village on a hill overlooking the City. From there you will get a good view of the whole urban area and beyond, you can see the Kentish hills to the east, as well as farms and great houses to the west. If you go to the adjacent Hampstead hill and look south east, you get an amazing view, almost as far as Dartford.

The City of London

The City of London is still surrounded by a wall which is over 2 miles long with eight gates (Tower, Aldgate, Bishopsgate, Moorgate, Cripplegate, Aldersgate, Newgate and Ludgate). In addition there is access via London

Bridge and by boat from the river. There is a postern near St Bartholomew's Hospital and a breach in the wall close to the river near the Bridewell house of correction. Close to three of the gates (Aldgate, Bishopsgate and Aldersgate) and near to the wharf at Billingsgate are churches dedicated to St Botolph – he is the patron saint of travellers and his churches are normally built on the outskirts of towns, just outside the walls. The old City stretches from the Tower of London in the east to Fleet Street in the west. The end of the City's jurisdiction is marked by Temple Bar, a gateway at the place where Fleet Street ends and The Strand begins. The main artery from west to east starts at St Paul's Cathedral and goes along Cheapside to Cornhill, Leadenhall and Aldgate. The main south to north axis is along the line of Gracechurch Street, Bishopsgate, Norton Folgate and Shoreditch High Street.

The City has spilled beyond the walls with housing in Aldgate to the east and around West Smithfield and Clerkenwell to the north west. John Stow described the growth of housing east of the City with many small houses being built in Wapping, Ratcliff, Poplar and Shadwell, while the street from Aldgate to Whitechapel was 'pestered with cottages and alleys even up to Whitechapel Church and beyond it, into the common fields which ought to be open and free for all men'.

Because the City is the financial and commercial district, the houses are built to meet the needs of merchants. They are typically two rooms deep and three or four storeys high with a shop and workshop on the ground floor, a parlour and kitchen on the first, bedrooms on the second and a small garret and store room at the top.

The biggest change the City has seen in the past eighty years has been the dissolution of the religious houses. All the priories, monasteries and colleges of priests in London have been closed down and sold off by the Crown. Many have been demolished or converted to other uses. For example, the Cistercian monastery next to the Tower was pulled down and the site was partly used to build small houses, but also large storehouses for victuals and ovens for baking biscuits for Her Majesty's ships.

Move to the West

As recently as Henry VIII's reign, the City was still a respectable place for aristocrats to live, but in the past sixty years, they have mainly sold up and moved towards Westminster. In Henry VIII's time, although the Tower of London was no longer used as a royal residence, the king built a new palace, the Bridewell, which is on the west side of the City. During his reign, a number of aristocrats acquired former monastic property which they converted into elaborate houses. However, by Elizabeth's reign the aristocrats had decided that the old city was too noisy, smelly and cramped and a fashion developed for moving into large houses much nearer to the court at Whitehall.

The typical fate of a former monastery in the City of London was that it would be acquired by an aristocrat and converted into a grand house, then sold by his descendants to a City merchant who would live in it. The Priory of Tortington in Sussex had owned a property with a large garden near St Swithin's Church but this had been acquired by the Earls of Oxford at the dissolution and renamed Oxford Place. By Shakespeare's time it belonged to John Hart, an alderman. Other large houses were sold for redevelopment. For example, a large property called Cold Harbrough near the Thames had been acquired by the Earls of Shrewsbury in the sixteenth century but was later demolished and replaced by a number of small tenements which, according to Stow, 'are now letten out for great rents to people of all sorts'.

Southwark

London lies along the River Thames; across the river is Southwark. This is now administered by the City of London and has been since 1550, but it is a very different sort of place. There are no respectable merchants with their shops full of dazzling displays of merchandise. Instead, there are taverns, ale houses, prisons, theatres, bear-baiting pits and brothels. Close to London Bridge is an area known as the Liberty of the Clink which is administered by the Bishop of Winchester and it is home to theatres and other places of entertainment. Further west is Paris Garden, an area that had originally belonged to the Knights Templar and is also home to a theatre. To the south of the Clink are St George's Fields where there is a windmill. In Shakespeare's *Henry IV, Part II*, Justice Shallow says, 'O, Sir John, do you remember since we lay all night in the windmill in St George's Fields?'

Gardens

Surprisingly, London still has a number of large gardens. The houses of the aristocracy on The Strand have gardens going down to the river and there are some large houses in the City that still retain their gardens, notably Fisher's Folly in Bishopsgate, which was built by Jasper Fisher who could not afford it and so it became the residence of the Earl of Oxford. The Inns of Court have fine gardens – in 1583, a survey of trees in Gray's Inn showed ninety-one elms, three walnuts and one ash. The gardens favoured in England have little of the natural about them, being heavily designed. Scented flowers are popular, as are shaded arbours and walkways. A mount with a summerhouse on top is fashionable, as are knots – a symmetrical design made from rosemary, thyme or hyssop, with the spaces between the plants filled in with coloured earth. Flowers are important in people's houses – the floors are strewn with rushes and the corners are filled with nosegays – and sometimes there are troughs for plants near the windows.

John Gerard is the great London herbalist and plant expert. He has a large garden in Holborn where he grows exotic plants and he looked after Lord Burghley's garden. He runs the Physic Garden, which belongs to the Royal College of Physicians. Queen Anne leased a 2-acre garden near Somerset House in The Strand to him. His *Herball*, published in 1597, is very popular and comprehensively illustrated with woodcuts; the book gives information about where the plants are to be found and how they are to be cultivated, as well as their medicinal and culinary uses. Many of the plants he describes grow in his garden or in the fields north of London, while he also gives the first published descriptions in English of many plants from North America, notably the potato.

Getting About

The streets of London are notoriously crowded, mainly because of the number of vehicles. Stow said that there was a large number of cars, drays, carts and coaches and that these were very dangerous: 'the coachman rides behind the horses tails, lasheth them and looketh not behind him; the drayman sitteth and sleepeth on his dray and letteth his horse lead him home'. There are constant complaints about the behaviour of the drivers of carts. According to Horatio Busino, among the carts on London's roads 'are some very filthy ones, employed solely for cleaning the streets and carrying manure, and it is precisely the drivers of these who are usually the most insolent fellows in the world'.

Busino paints a vivid picture of the waggons that bring people and goods into London: 'four wheeled waggons come up from the country bringing goods and passengers higgledy-piggledy, precisely like Maghera boats and they are drawn by seven or eight horses in file, with plumes and bells, [and] embroidered cloth coverings'.

According to Stow, the problem of congestion was made worse by the increasing fashion for private coaches: 'but now of late years the use of coaches, brought out of Germany, is taken up, and made so common, as there is neither distinction of time nor difference of persons observed: for the world runs on wheels with many whose parents were glad to go on foot'.

Fynes Moryson, writing in 1617, shared the same view: 'sixty or seventy years ago, coaches were very rare in England, but at this day, pride is so far increased, as there be few gentlemen of any account (I mean elder brothers), so as the streets of London are almost stopped up with them'.

This use of private coaches is a sign of increasing prosperity. Coaches cost a lot to buy, usually over £30, but cheaper second-hand ones are available; added to this is the cost of employing a coachman and fodder for the horse. But, for those lucky enough to be able to afford one, they do offer the luxury of privacy – something rare in a world where lives are led pretty much in the open. In *The Merchant of Venice*, Portia say to Nerissa, 'but come, I'll tell thee all my whole device when I am in my coach which stays for us at the park gates'.

One problem is that drivers of carts refuse to make way for each other if they come face to face in a narrow street and they park their carts wherever they fancy with no regard to the traffic. The carts are also noisy, particularly if not maintained; they squeak and creak and those that have wheels bound with iron make a loud noise and damage the road surface.

There are particular problems round London Bridge which is very narrow and is constantly congested and this spreads to the surrounding streets. According to Grenade, Thames Street 'is often blocked up that sometimes passers-by are brought to a standstill for a long time'.

The Common Council of London is trying to improve traffic flow. In 1586, they introduced a set of rules forbidding carts from being left in the street overnight or from waiting other than at specific parking places. Carts had to be driven at a normal pace and not to speed. Their drivers had to look out for children and old people and there were fines for drivers of carts which were noisy because they had not been greased or had wheels shod with iron.

Sadly, these good intentions seem to have been ineffectual. In his *Survey of London*, published in 1598, John Stow said:

> I know that, by the good laws and customs of this city, shod carts
> [i.e. ones with metal bound wheels] are forbidden to enter the same,
> except upon reasonable cause, as service of the prince or such like,
> they be tolerated. Also that the fore horse of every carriage should be
> led by hand; but these good orders are not observed.

In 1617 the Common Council was well aware of the rude and disorderly behaviour of carmen, draymen and others and they tried to improve the traffic flow by creating new places for carts to wait and introducing a sort of one-way system around Thames Street. But these efforts have not been too successful, because, in 1618, King James, when knighting one of the lord mayors, told him that he had to deal with two issues – the little devils, which were the apprentices, and the great devils, which were the carts that in passing along the streets did not choose to yield or give way to the coaches of the gentry when they met them.

For many people the obvious way to get around London is to use the river. It is particularly useful if you want to avoid the congested London Bridge or to travel upstream or downstream. In addition, the river taxis will drop you nearer to your desired destination at one of the many stairs along the banks. There are about 3,000 watermen, many of whom live in Southwark. They provide a taxi service using large rowing boats called wherries. Some speed along with two watermen each rowing with one long oar beating the water. Others are rowed by a single oarsman handling two shorter sculls on his own. The fares on the river are regulated – it is a penny to go across, 2*d*. to go from Temple to Westminster and 3*d*. to go from Blackfriars to Westminster. An additional 50 per cent is charged if you want to go against the tide and tipping is essential – the watermen have a reputation for being rude to people who fail to tip them sufficiently. Many visitors find a trip in a wherry a pleasant experience. Thomas Platter said: 'The wherries are charmingly upholstered and embroidered cushions laid across the seats, very comfortable to sit on or lean against, and generally speaking the benches only seat two people next to one another; many of them are covered in, particularly in rainy weather or fierce sunshine. They are extremely pleasant to travel in.'

Alessandro Magno really enjoyed the river. He described the wherries: 'they have no cabins, but sometimes they put cloths up to act as canopies when necessary and one man alone can steer them with two oars. The boats are broad at the back but dart quickly hither and thither across the river, according to the whims of those inside.' He also described larger boats used by groups of people to travel to different places or to simply enjoy themselves on the river in the evenings. He concluded that 'it is just as pleasant as it is to go along the grand canal in Venice. Upstream of the bridge there is a wide and very fine view of beautiful palaces and gardens and many boats go there for pleasure.' From the river at Westminster he saw 'fine great houses made of stone like castles, parks with deer, places for rackets and bowls and pleasure gardens and fountains'.

However, there is one dangerous spot on the Thames and that is London Bridge. The bridge has narrowed the river and a great volume of water has to pass through its arches. As a result, going under London Bridge when the tide is flowing out very swiftly can be a scary and dangerous experience. Thomas Platter described the problem: 'Below the bridge the river falls away so that when it is at its lowest and the tide is out, it is extremely dangerous to pass through; if, however, due to the incoming tide the river has risen, one may still feel a drop in this level, but now without danger'.

Another attraction of going on the river is the large number of swans that can be seen. These are often mentioned by foreign visitors. Alessandro Magno said:

> No less remarkable are the many swans that swim in the river. They are so domesticated that they take food from men's hands, as amongst us the more tame animals do. This is the reason, I believe why men treat them with so much respect: there is a law amongst them that anyone who kills a swan is bound to pay a fine to the Queen.

As well as the swans, it is also possible to see the king's royal barge with its two splendid cabins, glass windows and painted and gilded exterior. This is kept on the south bank of the river near the theatres.

Although London is a large and crowded city, the authorities do their best to ensure that it is as clean as possible. Householders have to wash the streets outside their houses. They leave their rubbish in the streets, but it is then picked up by dung carts three times a week.

Going to Church

Although England is strictly Church of England, there is provision for those of other denominations. Catholic visitors from overseas can attend Mass at the houses of the Spanish or French ambassadors (though any English person who attends will likely be arrested). There are Dutch and French Protestant churches. The Dutch one is in the former church of the Augustine Friars in Broad Street, while the French is in the former hospital of St Anthony in Threadneedle Street.

Travelling Outside London

Many foreign visitors like to see some of the sights outside London, including Nonsuch Palace, Hampton Court, Windsor, Oxford and Woodstock Palace. In 1599, Thomas Platter and friends hired a coach which took them to Hampton Court, then the 6 or 8 miles to Windsor and then to Wycombe, Tetsworth and eventually to Wheatley, where they stayed the night. The next day they went on to Oxford, where they stayed two nights at the Bear and visited the royal palace at Woodstock. On the way back they had lunch at Tetsworth and spent the night at Beaconsfield and arrived in London the following day. It is about 44 miles from London to Oxford and is a two-day journey by coach. Others prefer to go north east of London and visit Lord Burghley's house at Theobalds with its wonderful gardens which include a mount, a labyrinth and a fountain. From there it is possible to continue on to Cambridge.

Tourists often hire coaches because they are relatively comfortable and it is easier to carry luggage. Thomas Platter's trip to Oxford cost him 16*s.* a day for coach hire, including the coachman, horses and the carriage itself. The problem is that coachmen will not normally travel more than two days' journey from the City because the roads are very bad. Platter's original plan had been to go from Oxford across country to Cambridge, but the coachman refused because of the poor conditions of the roads, which were boggy and difficult to find, and the risk of damage to his carriage, which had problems with one of its wheels. Platter appealed to the Chancellor of Oxford University who sought the advice of two blacksmiths, but eventually came down on the coachman's side.

Where to Eat

There are a number of different types of hostelries in London. At the bottom of the heap are ale houses – these are usually small establishments and sometimes have a poor and rough clientele. One step above these are the taverns which are slightly more respectable. Thomas Platter described how in taverns 'it is the custom to erect partitions between the tables so that one table cannot overlook the next'. Above these are inns which have rooms for accommodation and stabling for horses. In addition, there are establishments called ordinaries, eating places that sometimes offer better food than inns. However, these vary in quality and in the type of people they attract. Some are for gentlemen, while others are for merchants and others attract a rather dangerous and shifty clientele of thieves, cutpurses and masterless men. You should seek advice from the landlord of your inn or fellow countrymen before deciding which ordinary to visit.

Where to Stay

There are very many inns in London and the towns where visitors like to stay, but it is worth bearing in mind that foreign visitors sometimes complain that English inns are expensive and that the food is not great. Fynes Moryson reported, 'I have heard some Germans complaine of the English Innes, by the high way, as well for dearenesse, as for that they had onely roasted meates'. He said that they had probably landed at Gravesend and been fleeced by those knaves 'that flocke thither onely to deceive strangers, and use Englishmen no better'. There are a number of inns in London that are owned by people from France or the Netherlands and these tend to attract visitors from their own countries. When Thomas Platter, a Swiss medical student, visited in 1599, he stayed at a tavern called The French Lily in Mark Lane, run by a Frenchman, Monsieur Briand. Similarly, Alessandro Magno, a Venetian who visited in 1562, stayed at the Ball Inn (Della Balla), run by an Italian, Master Caludio, and was very pleased with the service he received there.

The views of travellers about English inns vary considerably. Paul Hentzner described how he stayed at an inn in Rye 'where we were very well entertained as one generally is in this country'. Alessandro Magno said that 'the inns are very clean and they treat very well any who go there'. Thomas Platter was concerned about the charges in taverns that did not offer an all-inclusive price for a meal and where customers have to pay for each item separately: 'indeed it works out very dear for one person alone desirous of making a good meal and drinking well'.

Fynes Moryson, who has travelled extensively across Europe and into Turkey, believes firmly in the superiority of the English inn: 'the world affords not such Innes as England hath, either for good and cheape entertainement after the Guest's owne pleasure, or for humble attendance on passengers even in very poore Villages'. He explains the procedures at an inn. On arrival a servant will take your horse and walk it around until it is cool. He will then feed it. A second servant will show you to your room and light a fire. A third servant will remove your boots and clean them. The host of the inn will then come and ask you what you would like to eat. There are two choices regarding how to take your meal. Either you can dine with the host and hostess or with other people in the inn – this is usually cheaper and you can get a reasonable meal for about 6d. Alternatively, you can eat in your room, in which case you simply tell the host what you would like to eat and how you like it cooked and it will be prepared for you. The musicians will offer to play for you, but this is not compulsory.

Moryson has some useful advice for those staying in inns. First, it is much cheaper if you eat in a group, rather than dining alone. Second, he says that you need to be very careful about how your horse is looked after and take care that it is properly fed by the staff of the inn. Finally, he says that it is important that you check your bill carefully, as the staff of the inns may try to cheat you. In terms of meals, he says that it is normal to keep some of the food served at supper time for breakfast. Some people who are travelling will have two meals a day – breakfast when they set off and supper when they arrive.

Good inns for travellers can be found near St Helen's Church in Bishopsgate. According to Stow the area has 'diverse fair inns large for receipt of travellers', including one at the sign of the Dolphin. He also mentioned two taverns in Cornhill, the Pope's Head and the Cardinal's Hat, the Saracen's Head near Smithfield and another large inn near Cheapside called Blossom's Inn, or, as the cockneys call it, Bosom's Inn. There are also a number in Bread Street, also near Cheapside.

There are a vast number of these establishments, Thomas Platter said, 'There are a great many inns, taverns and beer gardens scattered about the

City, where much amusement may be had with eating, drinking, fiddling and the rest, as for instance in our hostelry which was visited by players almost daily'. Horatio Busino commented that 'there are endless inns and eating houses for board alone or for board and lodging'.

Some London inns are famous because they are mentioned in Shakespeare's plays. Tradition and an oblique reference in *Henry IV, Part II* indicates that Falstaff and Prince Hal favoured the Boar's Head Tavern. Prince Hal asks Bardolph where Falstaff is:

> Prince Hal: 'Doth the Old Boar feed in the old frank?'
> Bardolph: 'At the old place, my lord, in Eastcheap'.

The reference to the inn is a slight anachronism by Shakespeare – there is a tavern of that name today, but it did not exist in Henry IV's time.

A number of inns have theatrical connections, aside from those that are used for putting on performances of plays. The Magpie near Houndsditch was owned by Edward Alleyn senior and his actor sons Edward and John were born there. Shakespeare seems to have given a bit of a boost to the Elephant Inn which was located in Southwark. In *Twelfth Night*, Antonio says: 'In the south suburbs, at the Elephant, Is best to lodge: I will bespeak our diet'. Shakespeare also mentions the White Hart in Southwark as the headquarters of Jack Cade's rebels in *Henry VI, Part II*. The Mermaid Tavern, at the junction of Bread Street and Friday Street, Cheapside is the home of a group of literary figures who meet there on the first Friday of the month to drink and exchange witty sayings. The group includes Ben Jonson, John Donne, Inigo Jones and Hugh Holland. Shakespeare certainly knows some of the group; the landlord of the Mermaid, William Johnson, witnessed a document when Shakespeare bought a property in Blackfriars.

Cockney Stories

Londoners have no sense of their own history. Partly this is due to the historian Geoffrey of Monmouth who produced a 'history' of the kings of

Britain in the twelfth century. Much of his history was made up, including the idea that Britain was settled by the Trojans, and he was dismissed as a fantasist quite early on. Giraldus Cambrensis, his contemporary, told the story of a man who was beset by demons. When they became too troublesome a copy of St John's Gospel was placed on his chest and they flew away. But if a copy of Geoffrey of Monmouth's book was placed there, they came back in larger numbers and stayed longer. Some of Geoffrey's ideas have found their way into popular history and so Londoners and others will tell you all sorts of nonsense.

Some of their stories centre on Julius Caesar, who, according to cockneys, built the Tower of London and, as Thomas Platter was told, also built Woodstock Palace near Oxford. Then there are stories about King Lud. Grenade who visited in 1578 was told that London was founded by a Trojan called Brutus who wandered the seas and came up the Thames where he founded a city which he called New Troy in honour of his birthplace. It retained this name until 68 BC when King Lud renamed it Ludunum in honour of his name. Ludgate was also named after him. King Lud is one of Geoffrey of Monmouth's inventions and so the city cannot have been named after this imaginary figure. The real origin of the name London is a mystery. Ludgate, however, is known to be derived from an old English word meaning postern.

The third set of stories that Londoners like to tell is about giants. These trace their origins back to Geoffrey of Monmouth who said that when the Trojans arrived in Britain the country was inhabited by a race of giants, including a most fearsome one called Gogmagog. Eventually, he was killed by Corineus, a Trojan ruler, who challenged him to a wrestling match and threw him onto rocks in the sea. Corineus became ruler of that part of England in which this fight took place and gave his name to the area – Cornwall. The giant Gogmagog may be related to the names Gog and Magog which appear in the Bible. Two giants called Gogmagog the Albion and Corineus the Briton greeted Queen Elizabeth at Temple Bar on her departure from the City after her coronation and they play a leading role in the Lord Mayor's parade every year. The two are increasingly coming to be called Gog and Magog and are seen as the guardians of the City.

However, they are not the only giants in London. In Basing Lane is a large house built of stone which is now a common hostelry for travellers. A large fir pole nearly 40ft long is kept there and the story is that it was a staff belonging to a giant called Gerrard who used to live there. Stow, who is not a big admirer of giants, thinks that, in reality, this pole is simply a maypole. Stow also described a huge shankbone (tibia) which is on display in St Mary Aldermanbury. He says, 'true it is that this bone from whencesoever it came, being of a man as the form showeth, must needs be monstrous and more than after the proportion of five shankbones of any man now living amongst us'. He is a bit more sceptical about the heavy thigh bone of a man that is on display in St Lawrence Jewry. He does not know its history 'and therefore, rejecting the fables of some late writers I overpass them'.

Even respectable people seem to lack a sense of history, or to have a very distorted one. There are many stories about Westminster Hall which is the place where the courts sit. One concerns its famous hammerbeam roof. Londoners believe that it is made from a special type of wood that does not attract dust, dirt or insects. Some claim it is made from sweet chestnut, which, they say, repels beetles and is unattractive to spiders. Others, such as John Norden, the famous map maker, believe the wood comes from Ireland, a reference to the story that St Patrick banned all vermin from that country. A similar story was told to Hentzner who reported that the furniture in the Parliament chamber was made of Irish wood which 'is said to have the occult property that all poisonous animals are driven away by it'. In fact, the roof of the hall is made of English oak.

Dick Whittington

One curious example of Londoners' love of fantasy stories that you may hear is the story of Dick Whittington. There is a play about him called *The History of Richard Whittington, of his lowe byrth, his great fortune* and there is also a ballad that is sung in the streets. The story is that Dick Whittington was a poor boy from the west of England who came to London because he had heard the streets were paved with gold. He was given a job as a scullion in the kitchen of a wealthy London merchant called Hugh Fitzwarren where he was badly treated by the cook, but Fitzwarren's daughter, Alice, befriended him. Fitzwarren sent a ship off on a trade expedition and all the members of the household were invited to contribute something that could be sold for a profit. All poor Dick had was his cat. Soon after the ship left, Dick got fed up with his miserable life and decided to go home, but as he reached Holloway, he heard the bells of London calling to him, saying, 'turn again Whittington, Lord Mayor of London'. Meanwhile, the ship had been blown off course to the Barbary coast where the king offered to buy its entire cargo for a sum of gold. However, the king's court was plagued with rats and mice and the crew introduced him to Dick's cat which slew the vermin and the king offered to buy it for more than he had paid for the rest of the cargo. When the ship returned home, Dick was a rich man, he married Alice, went into partnership with Fitzwarren and eventually became Lord Mayor three times just as the bells had foretold. When he died, he left all his wealth to the poor.

Unlike many London tales there are elements of truth in this. There was a real Richard Whittington who married an Alice Fitzwarin and was Lord Mayor of London in 1397, 1406 and 1419. He gave generously to the City, endowing a library at the London Guildhall, funding a refuge for unmarried mothers at St Thomas's Hospital, helping to pay for the rebuilding of the Guildhall and providing a large public toilet in the parish of St Martin Vintry. He left all his money to charity and his executors undertook a major programme of works, including rebuilding Newgate Prison, rebuilding the south gate of St Bartholomew's Hospital and installing drinking water fountains in the City. In fact, the real Whittington came from a family of minor gentry and got an apprenticeship as a mercer in London, his wife's father was a landowner and not a merchant and, worst of all, there is no record that he had a cat, but let us not spoil a good story.

Women

Foreign visitors often remark on the freedom enjoyed by English women; they notice that they can attend playhouses and the swearing-in of the

Lord Mayor. Thomas Platter said, 'what is particularly curious is that the women as well as the men, in fact more often than they will frequent the taverns or ale houses for enjoyment'. Women married to artisans often help with the family business and some take it over if their husband dies. Fynes Moryson quoted a proverb that said that England is the Hell of Horses, the Purgatory of Servants and the Paradise of Women; because the men there ride their horses without any restraint, treat their servants imperiously and their women obsequiously.

Risks

Like all cities, staying in London can be dangerous – there are ever present risks of disease, fire and crime. Being aware of these dangers will help you have a safe and enjoyable visit.

The biggest threat is plague. This terrible disease is spread by fleas from infected black rats. These rats (*rattus rattus*) are smaller than their brown cousins and are expert at climbing and getting into all sorts of spaces. For obvious reasons, they are also known as roof rats or ships' rats. A flea that has fed on an infected rat can go on to bite a human who will then catch the disease and 70–80 per cent of those who are infected die, most within a week. Plague can spread quickly within a household. Its symptoms are headaches, fever, vomiting, painful swellings on the neck, armpits and groin, terribly painful blotches caused by bleeding beneath the skin, coughing up blood and dementia. It is the most terrifying disease, Thomas Dekker commenting it had 'a Preheminence above all others ... none being able to match it for Violence, Strength, Incertainty, Suttlety, Catching, Universality, and Desolation. It is called the Sickness, as if it were the onely Sicknesse, or the Sicknesse of Sicknesse, as it is indeede.'

Plague comes to London about every ten years and there have been major outbreaks in 1563, 1592–4, 1603 and 1608–10. It is normally only a problem during the summer months, roughly between April and September when the fleas are active. The disease can have a huge impact on society: between a quarter and a third of London's population died in 1563. Theatres and places of entertainment are closed during the outbreaks.

Ways of preventing the disease are based on the observation that the smell of decaying rubbish seems to infect people and consequently it is believed that strong smells can provide immunity by overcoming the foul air. People like to make embrocations and nosegays and pomanders out of herbs such as rosemary, rue, lavender, sage, mint, wormwood and nutmeg. They place bunches of herbs at their doors and windows to ensure that only sweet air enters the building since it is believed to provide protection. Some claim that tobacco is a preventative as no tobacconist has ever died of the plague. These ways of preventing the disease are useless and some precautions used by the City authorities are harmful – they round up stray dogs and cats because they are believed to contribute to the problem – in fact, dogs and cats help to reduce it by killing rats.

The only thing to do if there are signs or rumours of the plague during your visit is to leave as quickly as you can. Speed is of the essence because many other people will try to get away and transport may prove a problem. During the plague outbreak of 1603–4, Thomas Dekker said 'there was not a good horse in Smithfield, nor a coach to be set eye on'.

Other diseases are common and some of London's water supply, particularly that which comes from the Thames, is quite polluted. There is more information about this in Chapter Two.

London's narrow streets and wooden buildings make it a natural fire trap and it is surprising that there have not been any really catastrophic fires for a long time. The biggest fire within the last 100 years was in 1512 which destroyed much of the Palace of Westminster. In 1538, there was a potentially serious fire in Rood Lane which led to the destruction of twelve houses and to nine people being killed. Three years later the house of Sir John Williams, the Master of the King's Jewels, caught fire, which, according to John Stow, led many of the king's jewels to be burnt and more embezzled. In 1561 there was a great thunderstorm over London and the Church of St Martin in Ludgate was struck by lightning and large amounts of stone fell into the street. While people were looking at this, they realised that the steeple of St Paul's Cathedral had also been struck and was on fire. The timber framework of the steeple and the roof of the nave were ablaze and a river of molten lead flowed from the roof down towards the river. Luckily the rest of the church was not too badly damaged and the roof was repaired, although the steeple has never been rebuilt.

The theatres in London are mainly quite temporary structures and can be risky places. In 1583 the gallery of the building on Bankside, which was used for bear baiting, collapsed on top of the audience, killing seven people and injuring many. In 1599, a house in St John Street in Clerkenwell, where a puppet show was being performed, collapsed killing five or six people and injuring between thirty and forty.

Guns are readily available in London and there have been some tragic accidents. In 1560, someone discharged a gun in the house of Adrian Arten, a Dutch merchant. This caused a barrel of gunpowder that was being kept in the house to explode, destroying four houses and killing eleven people. An equally horrific accident occurred in 1587 during a theatrical performance by the Admiral's Men. There was a scene in which a man was tied to a post and shot. Unfortunately, the gun used contained a real bullet. The actor fired, missed the man tied to the post and killed a child and a pregnant woman. Gunfire also resulted in the destruction of the Globe Theatre in 1613. A theatrical cannon used during a performance of *Henry VIII* set fire to the thatch and the wooden beams. Luckily, nobody was killed and the only victim was a man whose breeches were set on fire - they were soon put out with a bottle of beer.

Crime is the major concern of many visitors to a new city and London has a mixed record in this respect. At night, in the winter months, householders are required to place hanging lanterns outside their houses or in their shop windows between 6pm and 9pm ensuring the streets are well lit. In addition each parish has to provide watchmen who patrol the streets during the night hours. They are armed with vicious weapons – javelins, bills and halberds. The cries of the watchmen were set to music in Queen Elizabeth's day:

Give ear to the clock,
Beware your lock,
Your fire and your light
God give you good night
One o'clock

Later in the night they sing:

God give you good morrow, my masters
Past three o'clock and a faire morning

At 9 in the evening, the curfew is rung from the churches of St Mary-le-Bow, All Hallows, Barking, St Giles, Cripplegate and St Bride. One purpose of the curfew is to signal the end of the working day for apprentices and there have been disputes between them and the clerk of St Mary-le-Bow who rang the bell late. The youth of Cheapside made up a verse:

Clarke of the Bow bell with the yellow locks,
For thy late ringing thy head shall have knocks

The clerk replied:

Children of Cheap hold you all still
For you shall have the Bow bell rung at your will

Honest citizens who are polite to the guard can usually walk round at night. Visitors have commented on how safe they feel in London during the evening. Horatio Busino, who visited from Venice, said that 'one can really go about by night, unarmed and purse in hand'. James Howell, who visited Paris in 1620, remarked on how safe London was at night. He talked of 'the excellent nocturnal government of our City of London, where one may pass and repass securely all hours of the night if he give good words to the Watch'. Thomas Dekker gave some good advice about dealing with the guard in his *A Gull's Horn Book*: if you are approached by the guard, get one of your companions to address you as 'Sir' somebody and because the Guard respect titles they will let you go. Alternatively, 'counterfeit to be a Frenchman, a Dutchman, or any other nation whose country is in peace with your owne; and you may passe the pikes: for beeing not able to understand you, they cannot by the customes of the Citie take your examination, and so by consequence they have nothing to say to you'.

Not everybody thought that way. Shakespeare satirised the pompous and incompetent Dogberry of the Watch in *Much Ado about Nothing*. Lord Burghley had a real-life Dogberry incident in 1586 when in his coach on his way home from London to Theobalds. He told Sir Francis Walsingham that he saw groups of men standing outside ale houses holding long staves. He assumed they were sheltering from the rain or having a drink, but when he got to Enfield it had stopped raining and he realised they were members of the Watch. He approached one group and asked what they were doing and they said they were supposed to arrest three young men. Burghley asked how they would recognise the three men. '"Marry," said they, "one of the parties hath a crooked nose"; "and have you," quoth I, "no other mark?" "No" said they.' Burghley sent for the head constable and said to him, '"Surely sir, whosoever had the charge from you hath used the matter negligently; for these watchmen stand so openly in plumps [groups] as no suspected person will come near them, and if they be no better instructed but to find three persons by one of them having a hooked nose they may miss thereof."'

However, there are certainly risks if you walk about London. Pickpockets are notorious and operate in areas where there are large crowds. London's theatres are famous as haunts of prostitutes and cutpurses. There are women thieves too. In 1590, Elizabeth Arnold stole some jewellery and other goods from houses in Turnmill Street and passed them on to Elizabeth Hawtrey in Limehouse and Elizabeth Jonson in Westminster. All three were hanged.

The Moorfields area has bowling alleys and dicing houses and also its share of villains. Minstrels, ballad singers and other entertainers are sometimes used by pickpockets to attract crowds. A man called Barnes persuaded his sons to sing bawdy songs in some of the towns near London. A crowd would gather and while people watched the performance their purses and knives were quietly removed. Even more startling was the story of the street entertainer who climbed a steeple to distract people in the street while his accomplice, a cutpurse, got to work below.

Even the most respectable places are not without risks. On Christmas Day 1611, John Selman, dressed in very good clothes and looking like a gentleman, went to the chapel of Whitehall Palace when the king was present and stole a purse and 40s. Selman was caught and hanged, but at his execution another thief stole a purse from somebody in the crowd.

Pickpockets and cutpurses are often very well organised and sometimes work in teams. Typically, a person called a *stall* will isolate and manoeuvre a potential victim (the *cully*) into a position where the pickpocket (called a *foyster* or *lift*) will remove his purse which he will pass to a *snap* who will make a quick exit. Other pickpockets work with prostitutes (*trulls*) in an activity called *crossbiting*. The *trull* will lure the victim (the *simpler*) into an alley where he can be robbed, pickpocketed or blackmailed. Alternatively, she will invite the victim to a tavern for a pint of wine. After a time, a fierce-looking man with a huge beard will come in, pull out his dagger and ask the victim what he is doing with his wife or sister in a tavern. In order to pacify the angry husband, the victim is forced to pay a large sum of money. Other specialists are *nippers* who cut the straps that hold people's purses in place and then escape quickly. These criminals learn their trade from older experts. William Fleetwood, the Recorder of London, wrote to Lord Burghley in 1585 describing how he had found a school for pickpockets near Billingsgate. A pocket and a purse were hung up and bells were attached to them. The young trainees had to remove the money without making a sound.

Much useful information about the activities of these criminals and many like them can be found from a series of wonderful pamphlets that were very popular in Queen Elizabeth's reign and are still being written under King James. Their authors, Thomas Harman, Robert Greene, Thomas Dekker and others, describe the antics of London's rogues, confidence tricksters and other criminals. They also reveal some of the secret language called thieves' cant or peddler's French which is used by those who inhabit the underworld to hide their activities. There are many pamphlets and they borrow from each other shamelessly. Thomas Dekker said that they write these as 'entertainments to shorten the lives of long winters' nights that lie watching in the dark for us'.

They describe a world in which rogues are divided into strictly hierarchical gangs, each one of which is headed by an 'upright man'. People are inducted into these gangs by having a jug of beer poured over their heads and then they can learn the different specialisms of the gang – pickpocketing, stealing horses, cheating at dice and other villainies.

One of the main features of these pamphlets and something that all travellers to London need to be aware of is what is called coney-catching. Coneys are tame rabbits raised for the table, but in the world of Shakespeare's London they are naive young men, up from the country and ready to be skinned alive. The first stage in catching a coney involves young, smartly dressed men called *takers-up* or *fingerers* who haunt St Paul's, Christ's Hospital, the Royal Exchange or other fashionable places. They are on the look out for young gentlemen who have been sent to London from the country with the aim of learning the law or farmers who have come to see their lawyers. According to Robert Greene in his pamphlet *A Notable Discovery of Cozenage*, as soon as they see 'a plain country fellow, well and clearly apparelled, either in a coat of homespun or of frieze, as the season requires, and a side-pouch at this side – "there is a coney saith one"'. The next stage is to engage the coney in conversation – the *taker-up* is able to talk about farming or the law and pretty soon the coney is invited to a tavern to take a drink, where they bump into another smartly dressed man known as a *verser*. Later a third man called a *barnard* arrives and he appears to be drunk and begins to spend lavishly, buying a pint of wine. After a time he offers to teach the coney a new game he had just learned. The coney, befuddled with drink, is persuaded to play cards or dice. The game starts with low stakes – a drink, then twopence, then the stakes gradually increase until the coney loses all his money. If the victim tries to escape without paying, a fourth member of the gang, called the *rutter*, is waiting at the door with a sword and dagger. Sadly, it seems to be the case that employees of taverns and inns are sometimes associated with these villains and it is well to be cautious about letting them know where you are going and whether you have money.

As well as pickpockets and coney-catchers, London is full of a whole galaxy of other rogues. The most likely ones you will come across are the false beggars. There are many different sorts – *whipjacks* are men who pretend to be shipwrecked sailors and to beg alms and *dummerers* who pretend to be dumb. *Counterfeit cranks* dress in dirty rags and pretend to have the falling sickness (epilepsy). They add a degree of verisimilitude to their acts by sucking a piece of soap which allows them to foam at the mouth when they have an audience. *Abraham Men* pretend to have been in Bedlam (the Bethlem hospital for the insane), they dress in rags, laugh, weep, sing crazy songs and dance wildly. When they approach someone, they will say 'Poore Tom is a colde'. The rantings of Edgar in *King Lear* sound very like the voice of an *Abraham Man*: 'Who gives anything to poor Tom? whom the foul fiend hath led through fire and through flame, through ford and whirlpool.'

Buying jewellery is also a risky business in London. The Goldsmith's Company is supposed to maintain the quality of gold and jewels and has strict rules – it is forbidden to set false jewels in real gold or to set real jewels in base metal. Any gold items that are sub-standard can be broken up. However, frauds are carried out. In 1608, Thomas Sympson, a goldsmith, was arrested for producing faked jewels. He was in the habit of dyeing crystals and then employing stone cutters to cut them into the shape of rubies and mount them in real gold or enamel mounts. Despite this unfortunate incident, Sympson remained a wealthy jeweller and died rich.

Matters have got worse because, in 1613, the Florentine glass worker Antonio Neri published his book *L'Arte Vetrania* which includes recipes for imitation jewels called 'pastes'. These are very realistic and are made from glass with a high content of lead and some potash and soda.

It is not always possible to know what you are getting. Jewels from the East: amethysts, emeralds, topaz, garnets and pearls are called 'orient' and are more valuable than those from the Americas, but ones mined in the New World are sometimes sold as 'orient' jewels.

But do not be discouraged. London is one of the leading shopping and tourist centres of Europe and virtually all the visitors who come here say that they have had a great time.

Chapter Two

Eating, Drinking and Shopping

If you ask a visitor to England about food and drink, they will tell you about three things – the meat, the beer and sugar. They will also mention tobacco which is a major addiction for Londoners. If you ask them about shopping, they will tell you that London offers the best shopping experience in northern Europe.

Meal Times

In England, breakfast is a small meal, usually bread and a little meat; many people do not bother with it and it is not served at court at all. The main meal of the day is at 11am if you are a nobleman, gentleman or scholar. Ordinary Londoners and merchants eat at 12 noon after New Change has closed for business. Lords and gentlemen have supper at 5pm and merchants and ordinary Londoners eat an hour later.

If you are visiting London, then you must bring your own knife with you, because knives are not supplied. Spoons are often provided. The English do not follow the foppish Italian custom of eating with forks, which are reserved for eating fruit or sweetmeats. People usually share dishes of food which are called messes. You have to spear the meat or vegetables using your knife and then eat it using your fingers. You will be provided with a plate called a trencher. This will either be made from stale bread, wood or pewter with a small indentation for salt. Hygiene is very important and you will have to wash your hands before and after eating and between courses, using scented water. You also need to use a napkin to keep your lips and chin clean. Contrary to what you may have read, people do not chew meat off the bone – bones are placed into waste dishes called voiding dishes. Nor are there any dogs or even cats present at the meal.

If you are lucky enough to be invited to a wealthy household, you will find that there is a huge emphasis on luxury and display – there will be fine linen tablecloths and napkins and elaborate silverware bowls, dishes, plates, flagons and spoons. You will be provided with a silver or pewter plate, cup, spoon and loaf of bread. In the wealthiest households, you will not be given a glass or cup but will call for one from a servant when required. You will be seated in order of precedence. People at the top table and the more influential ones at the lower tables get better food. After the main meal, if you are sufficiently important, you will be invited to go to another room for what is called a banquet – a dessert of sweetmeats and fruit. Some large establishments have elaborate banqueting houses – at Lacock Abbey and Longleat they are built on the roof to allow the guests to enjoy the view. Lord Burghley had an ornate garden for banquets at Theobalds with a ditch in which you could go in a boat past the plants, a summer house with statues of twelve Roman emperors, as well as cisterns full of fish. While you are enjoying your banquet, the servants will have rushed into the main dining hall to enjoy their meal.

Typically, a meal in London starts with pottage which is the staple diet of the English – virtually everybody has it at least once a day. This is a vegetable stew which is often thickened with oats or barley or sometimes peas. Poorer people flavour it with onions, garlic or herbs, while richer people can afford spices and they can also add meat. There is a delicious recipe for a pottage containing almonds, wine, ginger, cinnamon and saffron.

Many foreigners who come to London remark on the eating habits of the English. They all agree that roast meat is England's favourite food. Hentzner said that the English 'devour less bread but more meat which they roast to perfection'. Alessandro Magno commented:

It is extraordinary to see the great quantity and quality of the meat – beef and mutton – that comes every day from the slaughter – houses in this city … Truly for those who cannot see it for themselves, it is almost impossible to believe that they could eat so much meat in one city alone. The beef is not expensive and they roast it whole in large pieces. Apart from chickens and other birds which one finds everywhere, they have many swans, much game and rabbits and deer in abundance.

Fridays and Saturdays and the whole of Lent and Advent are fast days where no meat may be eaten and so Londoners have to rely on fish. Luckily, fish are caught in the Thames and brought by boat to Billingsgate. Oysters from the Thames and Medway are popular while poorer people have to rely on stockfish. This is air dried cod which is imported from Norway and sometimes Russia. It has to be beaten with a wooden hammer and soaked in water before it can be eaten.

Bread is commonly eaten with meals, although less so than on the Continent, and its quality varies according to how much money a person has. The poor eat bread made from wholemeal flour which can be heavy and dense. Richer people eat white bread called manchet which is made from sieved white flour.

Vegetables are becoming increasingly fashionable and there is an amazing range of produce available – beans, cabbage, carrots, gourds, navewes (rape roots), pumpkins, parsnips, peas and turnips. There are also more exotic products, including potatoes and sea holly, which were believed to be aphrodisiacs. In Shakespeare's *The Merry Wives of Windsor*, Falstaff says:

> Let the sky rain potatoes;
> let it thunder to the tune of Green Sleeves,
> hail kissing-comfits and snow eryngoes [sea-holly],
> let there come a tempest of provocation.

There were also two types of samphire available, marsh samphire, which is a slightly salty and glutinous vegetable picked off salt marshes, and rock samphire, which grows on cliffs. Shakespeare describes the perils of picking this plant in *King Lear*: 'Halfway down Hangs one that gathers samphire – dreadful trade! Methinks he seems no bigger than his head. The fishermen that walk upon the beach appear like mice.'

Sweet potatoes are baked with sugar and spice in pies as a dainty dish for the table. Tomatoes have come from the New World, but John Gerard claimed in his 1597 *Herbal* that they are poisonous and so they are not usually eaten. Cauliflowers used to be rare delicacies being imported from Italy but are now grown near London. Indeed, the area round London now cultivates increasing numbers of vegetables for the capital. The dung and filth from the City's streets is carted out to the suburbs where it is buried in holes left by gravel digging and used to grow food.

The wealthy are fond of eating sallats. These are like salads, but include fresh, cooked and preserved items as well as flowers such as violets and marigolds. They vary from the very simple – shallots, radishes, boiled carrots, water parsnips and turnips, to very elaborate ones made for feasts. Gervase Markham gives a recipe in his book *The English Housewife* which includes almonds, currants, raisins, figs, olives, boiled eggs, capers, spinach leaves, oranges, lemons, pickled cucumber and cabbage leaves, all of which is dressed with oil, vinegar and sugar.

A variety of fruit is available – most is grown in England, although it has a very short season. Over the summer you may be able to enjoy gooseberries, cherries, strawberries, mulberries, raspberries, blackberries, bullaces, plums, damsons, apricots, strawberries, apples, pears, crab apples, peaches, filberts and medlars. Henry VIII's fruiterer, Richard Harris, was a real enthusiast and brought over various grafts from the Low Countries and France to improve the breeds of cherries and apples. Apricots also began to appear in Henry's reign. Not everybody enjoys English fruit, and Horatio Busino said that 'Apples are really very good and cheap of various sorts and procurable all the year round. The pears are scarcely eatable and the other fruits most abominable, their taste resembling that of insipid masticated grass.'

Busino had strong views about the way in which the English ate their fruit. He hated English cherries, but said that they were very popular, 'Gentlewomen go with their squires to the fruit and flower gardens and orchards to strive who can eat the most'. He also noted that 'they do not generally put fruit on the table, but between meals one sees men, women and children always munching through the streets, like so many goats, and yet more in the places of public amusement'.

Farmers and wealthier people often have dairies attached to their houses and sell cheese and butter. Traditionally, the profits of the dairy belong to the housewife who is responsible for managing it. Milk is not generally drunk in England, except by children and the elderly. However, whey – which is often called whigg – is one of the few non-alcoholic drinks that are safe to consume and it makes a good cool drink in the summer. Cream and other milk products are increasingly popular as part of the banquet. Sometimes sweetened cream will be served, or cream and eggs in which egg yolks are beaten into cream, the mixture is strained and then flavoured with sugar and rosewater. Syllabub is also becoming fashionable. This is made from a mixture of wine and cream which is served in little glasses with a spout at the bottom. The wine is drunk through the spout and the cream eaten with a spoon. Possets are also popular – these are made from sweetened and spiced milk which is curdled with wine or ale. It is a good remedy for a cold but was used by Lady Macbeth to drug the guards outside Duncan's rooms in Shakespeare's *Macbeth*:

> the doors are open, and the surfeited grooms
> Do mock their charge with snores. I have drugg'd their possets
> That death and nature do contend about them,
> Whether they live or die.

Water

London's water supply comes from three sources. First, there are wells found in a number of parishes, including the Clerk's well in Clerkenwell, the well called Dame Annis the Clear near Holywell and another well called the Perilous Pond in the same area. The latter got its name because several youths were drowned when swimming there. Second, a lot of water comes from springs outside London and is brought in through lead pipes called conduits. The most famous of these is the Great Conduit, which was built in 1237 and brings water from springs near Tyburn past

Charing Cross along The Strand and Fleet Street and across the River Fleet, past St Paul's Cathedral and then to a large cistern at the east end of Cheapside. Other springs near Paddington were fed into this in the 1440s. A much more modern conduit is Lamb's Conduit, which brings water from springs in Holborn to a cistern at the junction of Snow Lane, Cow Lane and Cock Lane. A lot of water also comes from the Thames. In 1582, a German, Peter Morris, built a pump near London Bridge to bring river water to various people's houses.

Running water inside houses is becoming more common and the royal palaces have supplies to their kitchens, wet larders, bathrooms and houses of easement. For those who do not have this luxury there are water-bearers who carry water from the cisterns to people's houses. A Welsh goldsmith and merchant called Hugh Myddleton is building a new river to bring clean water from springs near Ware in Hertfordshire to the citizens of London and many more people will be able to have clean running water in their houses. It is due to open in 1613.

Until the New River is built, there is a problem with getting water in London. The water from the conduits is clean and is used by people for drinking and cooking. The water is alkaline and so the lead pipes which are used to transport it rapidly become lined with chalk – there is no danger of lead poisoning. However, the water from the Thames is very unpleasant – muddy and with a distinct smell. Bed linen which is washed in it smells of river water.

Beer

While some water is safe to drink, most people rely on beer. This is made from barley cereal which is turned to malt by being soaked in water to encourage it to sprout and then heated to dry it out. The female flowers of hop plants are usually added to give it bitterness, but other flavourings, including roasted apples, nutmegs, ginger and sugar, are sometimes put in too. It is also sometimes served hot. The malt is used three times; first to brew a strong beer, then a weaker beer and finally a weak, bitter beer called small beer which is often given to servants. Many people brew beer at home, but usually buy their malt as it is complicated to make. Larger establishments often have separate brewhouses.

Beer has the advantage of being relatively sterile because the malt has to be boiled while the hops, which add flavour, also help to keep it fresh and have a mildly antibacterial effect. Because it is a natural process, brewing varies from season to season. In the winter it can be too cold to persuade the yeast to ferment the malt fully, while in the summer the beer can become sour and so beers brewed in March or October when the temperatures are not too hot and not too cold are the most popular.

It is drunk in a variety of vessels, pewter goblets for the more wealthy, while poorer people make do with earthenware mugs or stoneware flagons. English glass is becoming more popular, while Venetian-style glass is now being made in London.

Many visitors comment on the English taste for beer. Paul Hentzner said, 'the general drink is beer, which is prepared from barley, and is excellently well tasted, but strong, and what soon fuddles'. While Thomas Platter remarked, 'for the most part they drink beer which is as fine and clear in colour as an old Alsatian wine and very palatable, and is exported to far countries'.

Fynes Moryson reported that English beer was popular in Germany and the Netherlands. Others were less positive. Alessandro Magno said, 'the English also make a drink from barley and the seeds of hops which they call beer, healthy but sickening to taste. It is cloudy like horse's urine and has husks on the top.'

Cider and perry are drunk in Worcestershire, Kent and Sussex where cider apple trees are grown, while some people drink mead (made from fermented honey) or metheglin which is like mead but with added spices.

Wines and Spirits

Grapes for making wine are no longer grown successfully in England because the climate has become much colder since 1550 and there have been some famously cold winters. Thomas Platter tasted some wine grapes growing in Westminster and 'thought them rather watery and unfit for making good wine'. However, because London is the centre of an international trading market, a lot of excellent wine is imported. Duke Frederick of Wurtemburg said, 'if you want wine you can purchase the best and most delicious sorts, of various varieties, and that on account of the great facility which the sea affords them for barter with other countries'.

Keeping wine fresh is a problem and sulphur is sometimes added as a preservative while there are lots of tricks that can be used to revive tired or fading wine, including adding cheese or skimmed milk to white wine that is losing its colour.

Some wine merchants need to be carefully watched as they will try to trick you by allowing you to taste one wine but supply you with a different one. Watch out if they give you cheese or salty nuts before tasting, because these will confuse your palate.

Despite this, there is some good wine to be had. The wines of Cyprus called malmsey are very popular. They are made by harvesting the grapes late to concentrate the sugar. They are then dried on the roofs of houses for three days before treading and fermenting in earthenware crocks buried in the ground. This process produces a wine that is strong and sweet and very expensive, probably twice the price of other, less strong wines. As London is the centre of an international trading network, lots of different wines are available, including ones from Portugal, the Rhine, Gascony and, of course, Bordeaux, the claret of which has long been a favourite.

Shakespeare's anti-hero Sir John Falstaff ran a one-man marketing campaign for the wines of the Cadiz region in Spain with his famous speech on the virtues of sherry sack in *Henry IV, Part II*: 'If I had a thousand sons, the first humane principle I would teach them should be, to forswear thin potations and to addict themselves to sack'. There have been periods when sack was difficult to find because England was at war with Spain, but in 1587, Sir Francis Drake captured 2,900 butts or about 1½ million litres of sack during his raid on Cadiz, more than enough to satisfy Sir John.

Wine is expensive and highly taxed and so can only be afforded by wealthier people, as Fynes Morison noted, 'clowns and vulgar men drink only beer or ale but gentlemen carouse only in wine'.

The English also drink a curious spicy drink called hippocras, made from wine, sugar or honey and flavoured with cinnamon, ginger, nutmeg and sometimes cloves or peppers. It is normally served hot and is drunk at weddings, baptisms and at the end of large meals to aid digestion. Distilled spirits are also coming into fashion. These are called aqua vitae and are made by distilling the lees left in wine barrels or wine that is no longer pleasant to drink. Thomas Dekker wrote an account of a meeting of a gang of criminals at which they drank beer pepped up with the addition of aqua vitae.

Sugar

The wealthier English are, unfortunately, very addicted to sugar. This is used in all sorts of ways. It is added to drinks to sweeten them, while apothecaries make a range of lozenges and syrups consisting of sugar and herbs or fruits which are said to help with colds and digestive problems. In addition, sugar comfits containing caraway seeds or marmalades of quinces are served to help with digestion after eating. There is a fashion for sugar-based confections as the final course of large meals. These include fruit preserved in syrup, decorations such as knots and flowers made from a paste of fruit and sugar, candied fruit and flowers and fantastic creations from marzipan or spun sugar. Sometimes there are knives, glasses and cups made from sugar paste which can be used at table and then eaten. When Cardinal Wolsey entertained the French ambassador in 1527, his cooks made a virtual world out of sugar and marzipan with castles, St Paul's Cathedral, beasts, birds, fowls and people, some fighting with swords, some with guns, some vaulting and leaping, some dancing with ladies and some jousting with spears.

Sugar is expensive and to keep costs down, some people buy unrefined sugar in cones and then refine it by boiling it with dilute lime, clarifying with egg whites in oil, straining and drying – a lot of trouble to make something that rots your teeth. As a result of this addiction, many of the richer people have dental problems. Queen Elizabeth's teeth were black as a result of her love of sugar and the fact that she normally ate alone or with a few companions may have been because she had loose teeth.

Tobacco

This noxious weed came to England from the Americas in the 1570s where it seems to have been used for medical and religious or shamanistic purposes. However, in England it became fashionable to smoke, and Sir Walter Raleigh is claimed to have been the leader of this fashion. The English are far more addicted to tobacco than people from other countries. Horatio Busino, who came to London in 1617, recorded his impression of the popularity of smoking:

> One of the most notable things I see in this kingdom and which strikes me as really marvellous is the use of the queen's weed, properly called tobacco.... It is cut and pounded and placed in a hollow instrument a span long called a pipe. The powder is lighted at the largest part of the bowl, and they absorb the smoke with great enjoyment. They say it clears the head, dries up humours and greatly sharpens the appetite. He said that some people even keep a pipe by their pillows at night to gratify their longings.

Busino added that it was widely sold in most shops and that 'in my opinion no other country ought to introduce tobacco, for it enters cities with vapouring ostentation and then after being well pounded, departs loaded with gold, leaving the purses of its purchasers empty and their wits addled'.

Thomas Dekker does not approve and said that 'a Stinkard has the selfe-same libertie to be [at a theatre] in his Tobacco Fumes, which your Sweet Courtier hath'. King James has written a treatise, *A counterblast to tobacco*, in which he expresses his hatred of the smoking habit. He says it is 'A custome lothsome to the eye, hatefull to the Nose, harmefull to the braine, dangerous to the Lungs, and in the blacke stinking fume thereof, neerest resembling the horrible Stigian smoke of the pit that is bottomelesse'.

Shops, Markets and Fairs

Busino remarked how 'all the houses along the streets of the city, with the exception of some few palaces, are full of shops of divers artificers of every trade, and each house has its sign or mark like an inn'. He noticed how specialist shops tended to group together in particular areas:

> There is one quarter full of apothecaries' shops on either side of the way, besides others scattered here and there about the city; another is entirely inhabited by booksellers ... then there are the other streets of feather sellers, while certain mechanics make horn flowers and rosettes, as delicately wrought as if they were the finest cambric. There is a suburb of gunsmiths ... There are several falconers' shops whose proprietors do nothing at all but train birds of every sort for such as are fond of sport.

Thomas Platter said, 'Most of the inhabitants are employed in commerce; they buy, sell and trade in all the corners of the globe, for which purpose the water serves them well, since ships from France, the Netherlands, Germany and other countries land in this city, bringing goods with them and loading others in exchange for exportation.'

The gunsmiths and armour makers cluster round the Tower of London, the stationers and booksellers are found near St Paul's while the Royal Exchange and the shops on London Bridge are both fashionable shopping destinations. But there are other retail areas and street markets and fairs provide good opportunities for buying, while many goods are sold by street vendors.

The Royal Exchange

The greatest shopping mall in London is the Royal Exchange which was
founded by Sir Thomas Gresham. Gresham was the son of Sir Richard
Gresham who was a successful merchant, financier, dealer in former
monastic property and Lord Mayor of London. The Gresham family had
a business trading with the Netherlands which Thomas joined after he
left Cambridge. He was so successful that he was appointed royal agent
in the Netherlands in 1551, being responsible for the management of the
government's loans on the Antwerp money market. He acquired property
in London and had large estates in Norfolk.

During his time in Antwerp, he was very familiar with the bourse which
provided a place for merchants and traders to meet and do business. In
1564, his only son Richard died and, denied a link to immortality through
his descendants, he decided to immortalise himself in stone. In January
1565 he approached the Court of Aldermen of London and offered to
build a bourse if they would provide the land. The idea was accepted
and a site found on Cornhill and Gresham laid the foundation stone on
7 June 1566. Construction took two years and was managed by a Flemish
mason, Hendryck van Passchen. The London Bricklayers Company was
furious because Gresham was using Flemish construction workers. He
also imported stonework, wainscoting and slates from the Netherlands.

The Exchange consists of an open courtyard surrounded by an arcade
with a gallery full of shops above that. The arcade is paved with squares
of black and white marble. Around the courtyard are thirty-six columns
of dark stone 4m high which are decorated with coats of arms and bronze
images of the kings and queens of England. The first floor gallery is
surrounded by columns of jasper marble. There are entrances at the north
and south and on the south side there is an attractive turret with a bell.
Around the tower are two galleries where the City Waits singers perform
at 4pm on Sundays in the summer. Grenade heard them perform in 1578
and commented, 'the City Waits produce wonderful sounds at 4 o'clock
on Sundays when the days are long, to the great pleasure of the listeners
of whom there are very many'. In 1599, Randolphe Bulle was paid £35

plus a £15 bonus to make a clock for the Exchange with four faces and two figures to strike the quarter hours.

The Exchange is really two things in one building – a mercantile exchange and a shopping mall. The mercantile exchange takes place in the central courtyard (and the arcade if wet) where merchants come twice a day between 11am and midday and between 5pm and 6pm. The hours of the exchange are highly regulated – Mr Bulle's clock rings a bell when the hour for business starts and when it finishes. People from all the major trading nations with businesses in London – English, French, Flemish, Walloons, Italian and Spanish – come every day to trade. Their mail is delivered here and, most importantly, this is where they get intelligence from all round the world. According to Grenade, 'There also can usually be heard reports from many countries and regions, a great convenience for those who traffic and trade as much on this side of the water as beyond.'

The second role of the Exchange is as a shopping mall and the shops are arranged along the first-floor gallery. This is called the Pawn (from the Dutch word *pandt* or German *bahn* meaning street or passageway). The shops are very small – just over 1.5m wide and just less than 3m deep. They sell a huge range of goods – the largest number of shops are haberdashers selling ribbons, beads, purses, gloves, pins, caps and toys. Next come the mercers who sell velvet, silk and other fine cloths, there are also painter stainers who paint and decorate objects and cloth, as well as tailors and leather sellers. In fact, pretty much anything you might want to buy is available here. Do you need medical care, a bottle of wine, a book or would you like a legal document drawn up for you? All these and many more are available on the first floor of the Exchange.

The shops are highly individualistic and each one has a decorated sign, usually an animal, hanging outside. On the south side there is a veritable menagerie from squirrels to ferrets, a cat and mouse, a blue boar, an owl, a unicorn a male griffin and, most remarkable of all, a pleasant lion. A few are run by women, a number of widows of former owners as well as Helen Youth, a spinster, and Mary and Dorothy Hill, who took over from their father.

Business at the Exchange started slowly and on 22 January 1571, Sir Thomas Gresham was in a panic. Queen Elizabeth was due to pay a visit the next day, but quite a few of the shops in the Pawn were vacant. What to do? Gresham was desperate to put on a good show for the queen and he tried hard to persuade the shopkeepers who were present to stock up some of the vacant spaces with fine goods and wax lights so as to make a good display. He said that they could have the shops rent free if they would help out.

In fact, the visit was (mostly) a success. The queen, accompanied by the nobility, the French ambassador and Odet de Coligny, comte de Beauvais, who was a friend of Gresham, travelled from Somerset House along Fleet Street, Cheapside and past the Royal Exchange to Gresham's house in Bishopsgate for dinner. She sat at Gresham's table and ate two courses of various dishes and then she, Gresham and the most distinguished guests retired to another room for the 'banquet', a feast of comfits, sweetmeats, wine and distilled waters. Then she returned via the Royal Exchange and admired everything – she was particularly impressed by the shops in the Pawn and Gresham breathed a sigh of relief. However, he may have been a bit disappointed at what happened next. The queen instructed a herald to proclaim that in future the building should be called the Royal Exchange 'and not otherwise'. Gresham had spent a fortune on the building to guarantee his own fame and the queen had upstaged him.

However, the result of the queen's endorsement was remarkable and suddenly the Exchange became the most fashionable place to shop. Gresham who had struggled to fill the shops in the Pawn found he was able to double the rents. The shops became full of the finest goods the world could supply and attracted an international clientele.

Sadly, Gresham died in 1579. After his death, things began to go badly wrong at the Royal Exchange. He had married Anne Ferneley, the widow of the mercer William Read, who had two young sons from her first marriage. In his will, Gresham made a generous provision for Anne, leaving her an annuity of £2,388 a year, but made no provision for her surviving son by her previous marriage. The bulk of Gresham's estate went to the project designed to enhance his posthumous reputation.

He gave money for almsmen and to hospitals and prisons, but his major bequest was to set up Gresham College. This he did by transferring the ownership of the Royal Exchange to the City of London and the Mercers' Company. They received the rents from the shops in the Exchange and, in turn, funded lectureships at the college. Lady Gresham was furious and spent the remaining years of her life trying to overturn Gresham's will and doing as little as she could to maintain the Royal Exchange. The building began to attract a rough crowd – idle boys, beggars, cheaters and people of base quality. The Privy Council wrote to Lady Gresham warning her that 'the Queen will take great offence if so beautiful a building is allowed to decay'. Her death in 1596 made it possible for the City and the Mercers to take over the Royal Exchange and set up Gresham College as Sir Thomas had wished. The college has seven lectureships in divinity, astronomy, music, geometry, law, physic and rhetoric. Lectures are held daily (except Sundays). Each lecturer delivers a talk in Latin in the morning and English in the afternoon; the lectures are held in Gresham's magnificent house in Bishopsgate.

The Royal Exchange is a remarkable establishment. Its Flemish-inspired layout with its great courtyard, arcade and shops is definitely a Continental European building and very different from the other structures in London. It has also become a global shopping destination. According to Stow, originally the goods stocked were a bit miscellaneous and cheap – mousetraps, bird cages, shoe horns, lanterns, etc., but 'now it is as plenteously stored with all kinde of rich wares and fine commodities, as any particular place in Europe. Unto which place many forraine Princes dayly send, to be served of the best sort.' Clearly, Sir Thomas Gresham has achieved the posthumous fame he craved.

The New Exchange

One new and exciting venue has recently been opened in Westminster. This is Sir Robert Cecil, the Earl of Salisbury's New Exchange. Robert Cecil, who is the son of Lord Burghley and is Lord Treasurer, acquired some of the Bishop of Durham's property along The Strand and decided to use it to build a new shopping mall to rival the Royal Exchange. The location seems to be good – it is close to the aristocratic houses along The Strand, just down the road from Whitehall Palace and within a short walk of the Inns of Court. It is also much closer to the new fashionable areas of London to the west of the City than the Royal Exchange, which is a mile away.

Cecil's plans provoked fury in the City of London. The mayor and aldermen saw this as a direct competitor to their own Royal Exchange. The mayor wrote to Cecil complaining that 'it will have such advantages of our Exchange as will make it of no use at all ... and in time will draw Mercers, Goldsmiths and all other chief traders to settle themselves out of the City'. Cecil, who knew how to deal with angry officials, wrote a calming reply saying that he wished to leave the inhabitants of Westminster 'some such monument as may adorn the place and happily derive some effect of present benefit and future charity to the whole Liberty'.

Because of disapproval by the Londoners, Cecil decided to build his new shopping mall in double-quick time before they could take action to stop him. Stone was secured from all round the country; some came from the former monastery of St Augustine in Canterbury which was being demolished. The labourers worked six days a week with 2 hours overtime. As a result, it was finished in less than a year. The design is very like the Royal Exchange with an arcade where people can meet and do business as well as two floors of shops. The shops are very small and are about 1.7m deep, and are really the size of market stalls or kiosks. It is not surprising that the City sees this as a serious rival.

If Sir Thomas Gresham could get Queen Elizabeth to endorse his Royal Exchange, Cecil wanted royalty to support his new venture and so, on 11 April, 1609, King James, Queen Anne and their children, Prince Henry, the Duke of York (the future King Charles) and Lady Elizabeth, as well as many fine ladies and gentlemen came to the opening. Gresham had organised a dinner for Queen Elizabeth when she opened the Royal Exchange and Cecil decided to go one better. The guests were entertained by a show written by the noted playwright Ben Jonson with sets designed by the famous architect Inigo Jones. Rarities from India and China were on display and were offered to the king and distinguished guests. In what may have been an outburst of patriotic fever caused by the union between England and Scotland, Cecil gave his new shopping mall the name Britain's Burse.

The Exchange has got off to a slow start with only twenty-seven shops let by the autumn of 1609, but there are some smart milliners, linen drapers and haberdashers already in business and new lettings are expected.

Cheapside and Goldsmiths' Row

The most famous shopping destination in London is probably still Cheapside, although it has competition from the Royal Exchange and New Exchange. Also known as West Cheap, it runs east from St Paul's to Poultry and is the widest street in London, known for its fountains gushing water, inns, merchants' mansions and luxury shops. It is the site of one of the Eleanor Crosses. There are a whole range of different high-quality shops in this area which sell spices, haberdashery, ironmongery, millinery and leather goods. There are street vendors and market traders who sell poultry, milk, honey, vegetables, fruit and flowers.

The street was described by Grenade, who visited it in 1578:

The goldsmiths and changers on one side of the street number about 70 shops all in a row, full of all sorts of works and vessels in gold and silver alike, gilded or to be gilded. On the other side of the street are the great and magnificent shops, or rather warehouses, of all sorts of silken cloths. After these are the mercers, haberdashers, ironmongers, grocers etc. Finally there appear so many and such diverse varieties of wares on whatever side one turns to that it is a wonderful thing to behold, for it seems that not only Europe (signs of which are seen on all sides in this place), but also all parts of the world have attempted to try to make themselves known in London by sending to it the greatest rarities which are produced in their regions.

The main feature of this street is the goldsmiths' shops, and the area is really the Goldsmiths' quarter which occupies Cheapside and a maze of narrow passages, alleys and courts around West Cheap, as well as the surrounding streets to the south leading towards the river. The most famous row of shops is Goldsmiths' Row, which was described by John Stow in 1598:

> The most beautiful frame of fair houses and shops that be within the walls of London or elsewhere in England, commonly called Goldsmith's Row, betwixt Bread Street end and the cross in Cheap, but is within this Bread Street Ward: the same was built by Thomas Wood, goldsmith, one of the sheriffs of London, in the year 1491. It containeth in number ten fair dwelling-houses and fourteen shops all within one frame, uniformly built four stories high, beautified towards the street with the Goldsmiths' arms and the likeness of woodmen, in memory of his name, riding on monstrous beasts, all which is cast in lead, richly painted over and gilt. These he gave to the goldsmiths, with stocks of money, to be lent to young men having those shops &c. This said front was again new painted and gilt over in the year 1594.

The Goldsmiths are part of an international trade in gold, silver and precious stones and are very specialist, some make rings, other cut stones or make buttons or enamelled goods. Many of them come from overseas, attracted by the wealth of London, its religious toleration and political stability. In Cheapside, gem stones can be bought from all over the world, including emeralds from the Spanish colonies in South America, moonstones and sapphires from the island of Sri Lanka, rubies and diamonds from India and even turquoises from Afghanistan and malachite from Russia. If you run out of cash while in London, some goldsmiths will happily lend you money on the security of any gold or gems you are carrying.

Since about 1600, the number of goldsmiths in the area has declined. This is partly because of high rents, but also because their rich clients have moved away from the City and are now living in mansions along Fleet Street and The Strand. So goldsmiths have opened new shops in

Holborn, Fleet Street and The Strand to be nearer their customers and the court in Whitehall. Their place has been taken by milliners, perfumers, haberdashers, stationers, and apothecaries. King James is very unhappy about this and has tried to encourage the Goldsmiths' Company to find ways of persuading goldsmiths to return to Cheapside, but to little avail.

Opening hours – the goldsmiths are not allowed to trade after 5pm or to use candles (to prevent fraud), so shops close at 5pm in the summer and as early as 4pm in the dark days of winter.

St Mary-le-Bow

While in Cheapside, you should visit the Church of St Mary-le-Bow. This is the second most important church in London after St Paul's Cathedral. Its bells are famous and one is rung at 9pm every night to signify the curfew. They can be heard from as far away as Hackney Marshes.

The medieval church on the site was probably built in the 1080s, but in 1091, it was badly damaged in the London tornado and the roof was blown off and people died as a result. There were further disasters for the church – in 1271 the steeple collapsed, killing many people. The church gets its odd name because it is has two stone arches which are shaped like bows and so it was called St Mary-le-Bow. Stratford atte Bow in the east of London derives its name from the same idea – Stratford Bridge over the Lee consisted of three bow-shaped arches.

The church also attracted its fair share of criminals. In 1196, the church's steeple was seized by William FitzOsbert, a renegade tailor who fortified it and filled it with weapons and supplies. He and his accomplices were eventually driven out by the simple method of setting fire to the steeple. He was dragged by the heels to Smithfield where he and nine accomplices were hanged. At the last moment, he called on the Devil to rescue him. In 1284, the church was the scene of a real medieval murder mystery. It started when Laurence Ducket, a goldsmith, seriously wounded Ralph Crepin in West Cheap. Laurence fled into the church but Crepin's friends got inside in the night, killed Laurence and hanged him up to make it look as if he had committed suicide. An inquest decided he had killed himself and his body was dragged by the feet to a ditch outside the City where it was buried. Later, a boy who had hidden Laurence in the church came forward and told the story of the murder. Laurence's friends, including Jordan Goodcheap, Ralph Crepin and Gilbert and Geoffrey Clarke, were convicted and a total of sixteen men were drawn and hanged, and according to Stow, some others 'that being richer, after long imprisonment were hanged by the purse'. A woman called Alice 'that was the chief causer of the mischief' was burned. Laurence's body was eventually buried in the churchyard, but the church was closed for a time – its doors blocked up with thorns.

The Court of Arches sits in the church (hence its unusual name). The court deals with church matters and cases concerning wills and probate.

Other Shops

There are many other shopping districts in London, but first, a word of warning – don't get fooled by the street names. Many streets in the City have the names of the sort of shops that used to be found there in the Middle Ages, but in many cases no longer are. Many businesses have moved away from their traditional homes to other locations. John Stow said that the ironmongers had moved from Ironmonger Row to Thames Street, the Vintners had moved from the Vintry to various other places, the hosiers had moved from Hosier Lane to Cordwainer Street and Birchoveries Lane, the shoemakers had moved from Cordwainer Street to St Martin le Grand and the Poulterers had moved from Poultry to Grass Street and St Nicholas Shambles. Also, street names do not necessarily mean what you think. Pudding Lane is not a delightful street full of bakeries (although there is a bakery there), the name comes from the medieval word for the offal that would fall from the carts coming down the lane from the butchers in Eastcheap as they headed for the waste barges on the Thames. In Stow's words, 'the Butchers of Eastcheape have their skalding House for Hogs there, and their puddings with other filth of Beasts, are voided down that way to their dung boats on the Thames'.

Lombard Street, the origins of which go back to a grant of land to gold merchants from Lombardy by Edward I, is a very commercial shopping area with goldsmiths' shops, hosiers, drapers, mercers, booksellers, apothecaries and haberdashers, while Bucklersbury is full of grocers and apothecaries. Thomas Hobson has turned the former chapel of Corpus Christi and St Mary in Poultry into a warehouse with shops.

There are a number of different food shops spread through the City – poulterers, cheesemongers, pastry cooks, fruiterers and fishmongers. A range of fish is landed at Billingsgate and sold in the City – cod, ling, herring, pilchards, salmon and hake, as well as oysters, mussels and cockles. Cattle are driven down from Wales and the West Country and sheep from the Midlands to be fattened near London and sold in the meat markets and butchers' shops.

London is also famous for selling expensive clothes and there are many drapers' shops, notably in Watling Street and Candlewick Street (now Cannon Street), the latter having over 200 drapers' shops full of all sorts of cloths at all sorts of prices. It is also famous for the quality of its cutlery which is made by cutlers from overseas who have settled in St Martin le Grand. London coaches are world famous and are sometimes sent overseas to rich foreign buyers.

Markets

London is well furnished with markets and many citizens and their servants go there to buy food.

Opening Hours

Most markets are open from 6am until 11am and from 1pm until 5pm. Not all markets are open every day of the week. There is a limited Sunday service, only milk, herbs, flowers and roots can be purchased and these have to be bought before 7am (8am in the winter).

Where to Shop

Cheapside – general – poultry, butter, cheese, herbs, roots, fruits and spices, as well as saddlery, cloths, silk and textiles.

Cornhill – similar to Cheapside, but also sells rabbits, poultry, game, waterfowl and old clothes.

Bishopsgate – opened in 1599, selling malt, yarn and meal.

Queenhithe – grain.

Leadenhall – grain, poultry, eggs, butter, cheese and meat.

Billingsgate – mainly fish, also some grain, oranges, onions and fruit.

Old Fish Street – fish.

Stocks (outside the Royal Exchange) – fish and meat.

Newgate shambles – meat. The quality here is excellent. Grenade said that the meat here is not only overflowing with agreeable qualities and at the same time tender and of a delicate taste, but clean and also extremely well dressed.

Newgate Pavement – grain and general.

Gracechurch Street – food and grain.

West Smithfield – in the unlikely event you want to buy a horse or other animal.

Street Vendors

The streets are full of vendors, often women, selling a range of foodstuffs – oysters, mussels, salted fish, cockles and bread. They offer their wares six days a week, but are limited to selling 'timely' fruits (strawberries, cherries, plums, etc. which have a short season) on Sundays. Thomas Platter counted thirty-seven different commodities being cried in the streets of London in 1599. We are fortunate that some composers have set these cries to music and we are able to enjoy the cries of 'hott apple pies' or 'whyte cabbage, turnips, parsnips, lettuce and radish'. As well as a whole shoal of fish for sale, new oysters, fresh herring and:

> Sprats, sprats, sprats,
> Twopence a peck,
> At Milford Stairs.

Some street vendors approach kitchen maids hoping to buy unused foodstuff or waste materials and you can hear cries such as 'coney skins' or 'have you any kitchen stuff maids?' Others offer to exchange goods, one vendor offers to swap 'brooms for old shoes'.

As well as people selling food, there are a whole range of tradesmen seeking work – coopers, chimney sweeps and men offering to chop wood. If you need your shoes cleaning, listen out for this song:

> Buy any black, buy any black?
> Here cries one dare boldly crack
> He carries that upon his back
> Will make old shoes look very black
> Will ye buy any blacking maids?

Bartholomew Fair

When and Where to Go

The fair is held on three days in late August around the festival of St Bartholomew the Apostle and takes place in the former property of the Priory and Hospital of St Bartholomew, West Smithfield and the surrounding streets.

Grenade, who was there in 1578, described the event:

During this fair, the square of Smithfield and all the streets far around it, especially the square itself, is filled with so many tents, with a great abundance of all sorts of merchandise that one would think one was in the heart of the most mercantile city in Christendom. And during this time, one can see the beautiful wares of London, for everything is on display there.

The fair is a mixture of three things – a wholesale market, a retail market and a place for entertainment. The wholesale market is very important. In 1593, plague struck and although the retail and entertainment side of the fair was closed, the wholesale side continued with the bulk sale of cheese, butter, woollen and linen goods and, of course, horses and cattle.

There is a huge range of things on sale, including leather, cloth, pewter, livestock, butter and cheese. Food and drink is widely available with roast pig being regarded as the great delicacy. Toys are popular. In Ben Jonson's play *Bartholomew Fair*, Lanthorn Leatherhead, the hobby horse seller, calls out, 'What do you lack, what do you buy mistress? A fine hobby horse to make your son a tilter, a drum to make him a soldier, a fiddle to make him a reveller? What is't it you lack? Little dogs for your daughters or babies [dolls] male or female?'

There are plenty of entertainments – conjurors, actors, balladeers, wrestlers, tightrope walkers and fire eaters. There are also exotic animals. In *Bartholomew Fair*, one of the characters says he has been to see the eagle and the black wolf, and the bull with five legs and the dogs that dance the morris and the hare with the tabor.

Do be careful. In 1596, Paul Hentzner and his friends visited the fair where his companion, Tobias Salander, doctor of physic, had his purse picked from his pocket which, according to Hentzner, 'was without doubt so cleverly taken from him by an Englishman who always kept very close to him that the Doctor did not in the least perceive it'. In *Bartholomew Fair*, a cutpurse trips over a costermonger and upsets his pears. While one of the characters is scrambling to pick them up, he is relieved of his cloak and sword. The fair has its own system of justice with a court called a Court of Piepowder, a set of stocks, a whipping post and a ducking pond.

Chapter Three

Must-see Sights

When Grenade visited London in 1578, he wrote an account of the City and said he had 'observed in London four buildings of a wondrous structure and lavishness'. These were St Paul's Cathedral, London Bridge, the Tower and the Royal Exchange. These are certainly the most important sights of the City and ones that every visitor should go and see. The Royal Exchange is described in Chapter Two.

St Paul's Cathedral

The cathedral is by far the biggest building in London and is one of the biggest in the world. Sitting on the highest point in the City, overlooking the River Fleet and the Thames, it dominates the London skyline and (in the days when it had a spire) was visible 25 miles away. Even in these days when it does not have a spire, it is twice the size of the White Tower and 30m taller than the Eleanor Cross at the top of Whitehall. The lead roof is a spectacular sight rising 26m above the parapet and containing 397 tonnes of lead. The building looks rather like Salisbury Cathedral but is 30m longer and the spire 20–5m higher.

Londoners will tell you that it was built on the site of a temple to Apollo establishedby Brutus; alternatively that it was built by the Romans as a temple to Diana. The best we can say is that work on the building known to Shakespeare began in 1087 following a major fire which destroyed its predecessor. Royal support was given in the form of stones for the building while Henry I gave all fish caught in the neighbourhood and a tithe of all venison caught in Essex. Construction was delayed by a fire which broke out on London Bridge in 1135 and damaged the cathedral and the spire was not finished until 1221. Unfortunately, the new building was damaged by storms and in 1255 there was a major rebuilding project which included lengthening the church eastwards and by the end of the thirteenth century, the cathedral was pretty much in its final form.

The cathedral has always played an important role in the life of the nation. When Henry IV deposed Richard II, he had Richard's body displayed in the cathedral to demonstrate that he really was dead. The cathedral was the centre of enormous celebrations after the defeat of the Spanish Armada in 1588. The queen attended a service of thanksgiving and the building was draped with the flags and banners of the captured Spanish ships. In 1605, it was a more gruesome scene when four of the Gunpowder Plot conspirators were hung, drawn and quartered just outside.

Things to See

The aisle is huge and very splendid and equally fine is the rose window. There are a number of tombs that are worth looking at, notably those of two Anglo-Saxon kings (the only two kings to be buried there). One is of Sebbi, King of the East Saxons, who, towards the end of his life, abdicated and became a monk. He died in 695. The other is of Ethelred the Unready who was buried in 1016 and contains a terrible curse said to have been placed on him at his coronation by St Dunstan the Archbishop. Dunstan said that because Ethelred had succeeded to the throne after the murder of his brother 'the sword shall not depart from thy house, raging against thee all the days of thy life'.

As a result of the spread of radical Protestantism, many of the images and tombs have been damaged and defaced. Alessandro Magno, who visited London in 1562, said, 'It is a pitiful sight to see the beautiful marble statues of saints and other decorations there, broken and ruined because of their heresy.'

Probably the most famous tomb in the cathedral is that of St Erkenwald, the fourth Bishop of London. He was responsible for converting Sebbi to Christianity and he was a man of huge energy, strengthening the walls of London and building a new gate into the City – Bishopsgate. In the Middle Ages, there were regular pilgrimages to his tomb and special services on his day. His sister was Saint Ethelburga, whose church is close at hand. Unfortunately, like many other relics in the Cathedral, Erkenwald's tomb was damaged and the fine gold and jewel decorations removed during the Reformation of the sixteenth century.

The tomb of John of Gaunt, father of King Henry IV, is a prominent feature, while there are also some comparatively new tombs. The richly coloured marble tomb of Sir Nicholas Bacon, Queen Elizabeth's Lord Keeper of the Great Seal and father of the philosopher and scientist Francis Bacon, contains his two wives, Jane and Ann, was made during his lifetime. There are also the tombs of Sir Francis Walsingham, Elizabeth's spymaster, and Sir Philip Sidney, poet and soldier. The finest recent tomb is that of Sir Christopher Hatton which towers over the high altar. Hatton first came to Queen Elizabeth's notice because of his good looks and dancing skills, but eventually rose to be her Lord Chancellor.

A visit to the roof of the church is a popular Sunday activity for many people; Thomas Platter went there on his visit to London in 1599. Thomas Dekker in *The Gull's Hornbook* warned, 'take heede how you looke downe into the yard; for the railes are as rotten as your great-Grandfather' and explained that it was fashionable for people to scratch their names in the lead of the roof. However, some visitors from overseas feel they have been badly treated when visiting the roof. In 1617, Valentin Arithmaeus, professor of poetry at Frankfurt an der Oder, visited St Paul's. He wanted to climb the tower, but later grumbled, 'No German is admitted to it unless he pays his money beforehand, so intense is the avarice of the English'.

Many visitors enjoy the organ music in the cathedral. Platter comments on it, while Grenade said that the organ, which was built on the instructions of Henry VIII, makes a sound marvellous to hear when the chanters and children of the choir sing with it.

There was a small theatre in a room, the Almoner's Hall, on the south side of the cathedral, and plays, specially written by distinguished playwrights of the day were performed there by the boy choristers. The Paul's boys were in direct competition with a troupe of boy actors at the nearby Blackfriars. Unfortunately, the theatre closed in 1606 due to political pressure – the satirical plays for which they were well known were not acceptable to the censor.

Booksellers

The area round the cathedral – the churchyard and Paternoster Row – is famous for its bookshops and stationers. Book buying is popular with the rich and fashionable. In his satirical account of how wealthy newcomers to London should behave, Thomas Dekker said:

> I could now fetch you about noone (the houre which I prescribed you before to rise at) out of your chamber, and carry you with mee into Paules Churchyard; where planting your selfe in a Stationers shop, many instructions are to bee given you, what bookes to call for, how to censure of new bookes, how to mew at the old, how to looke in your tables and inquire for such and such Greeke, French, Italian, or Spanish Authors, whose names you have there.

A wide range of books is available – religious texts and bibles are popular, as are works of history, travel and topography. Richard Hakluyt's *The Principal Navigations, Voyages, Traffiques and Discoveries of the English Nation*, published in 1589, is well respected, as is John Speed's book of maps called *Theatre of the Empire of Great Britain*. Books on household management, herbals and gardening are also popular. Many of the booksellers around St Paul's and in Fleet Street sell individual copies of Shakespeare's plays. These are usually quarto-sized volumes and are pirated editions that are not authorised by Shakespeare and frequently contain errors. Some people suspect they are produced by getting scribes to take down the words of the plays in shorthand as they are performed, or else by persuading some of the actors to remember their speeches and dictate them to the publishers.

Outside the Cathedral

A number of features of the cathedral have disappeared in recent years. There used to be a separate bell tower with four large bells. According to rumour, Henry VIII gambled this away in a game of dice with Sir Miles Partridge who had the bells removed and melted down.

There also used to be a charnel house as well as a cloister, a chapter house and a chapel in the churchyard. Protector Somerset wanted the land for a park for his house by the river. As a result these were all demolished and the bones from the charnel house – about 1,000 cartloads – were taken to Finsbury Fields where they were piled up into a mound which was covered in earth and three windmills built on top. The area acquired the name Bone Hill and later became known as Bunhill.

St Faith and St Gregory

One curiosity of St Paul's is that it has another church underneath it. This is the Church of St Faith which served the area to the north of the cathedral. When the cathedral was extended in 1255, St Faith's was demolished and the parishioners were given a new home in the west end of the crypt. In 1561, they were moved into the Jesus Chapel at the east end. Most of the parishioners are booksellers and stationers who have shops in Paternoster Row. Surprisingly, there is also another church attached to St Paul's. This is St Gregory by St Paul which lies against the south wall of the cathedral. Like St Faith, it was built to serve the local parishioners.

Paul's Walk

St Paul's is on a direct line from Cheapside to Ludgate Hill and, as it has a door at each end, it has naturally become a short cut for tradesmen walking from one street to the other. It being dry and warmer than the streets, they stop and chat and so St Paul's has become a place where people naturally meet one another. The main aisle is known as Paul's Walk and it is a place where servants are hired, lawyers meet their clients and business is done. In *Henry IV, Part II*, Sir John Falstaff claims to have 'bought [hired]' Bardolph in St Paul's. Even out-of-work clergymen offered themselves for hire in the north aisle. Hiring servants in St Paul's was not always a great idea – there is a London saying that you should not make a choice of three things in three places, of a wife in Westminster, of a servant in Paul's or a horse in Smithfield.

Some idea of the behaviour of people in St Paul's is revealed in a proclamation by the Lord Mayor of 1554:

> Now of late years many of the inhabitants of this City of London, and other people repairing to the same have and yet do commonly use and accustom themselves very unseemly and unreverently; the more is the pity to make the common carriage of great vessels full of ale and beer, great baskets full of bread, fish, fruit, and other such things, fardels [bundles] of stuff and other gross wares through the Cathedral Church of St Paul within the said City of London, and some in leading of horses, mules or other beasts through the same unreverently, to the great dishonour and displeasure of Almighty God and the great grief also and offence of all good and well disposed persons.

There is another aisle in the cathedral that leads to a tomb that is widely believed to be that of Humphrey, Duke of Gloucester, the youngest son of Henry IV. In fact, this is another London fable – it is really the tomb of Sir John Beauchamp, while Duke Humphrey is buried in St Albans Abbey. Nevertheless, the aisle is known as Duke Humphrey's Walk and is a favourite haunt of beggars and insolvent debtors who loiter about looking for alms. There is a London saying 'Dining with Duke Humphrey' which means going without dinner.

Paul's Cross

Outside St Paul's is the famous Paul's Cross with its pulpit for preaching. Originally built in the Middle Ages, the current pulpit dates back to 1449. Every Sunday, a leading preacher delivers a sermon and this attracts large crowds. There is a building called the sermon house where the mayor and aldermen sit and listen to the talks. Very many famous preachers have spoken there and it attracts large crowds. One of the grandest and, in the end, most ironic occasions was in 1521 when Cardinal Wolsey and the ambassadors of the Pope and the Holy Roman Empire and all the bishops sat in great state to hear John Fisher, Bishop of Rochester, preach a sermon against Martin Luther. Little did Wolsey and Fisher realise but a few short years later both would be accused of treason. One would die before he could be tried and the other would be executed at the Tower.

London Bridge

London Bridge is a constant surprise to foreign visitors who are all impressed by its length and its structure with rows of shops on either side. Grenade said, 'there is no bridge in the whole of Europe which is on a great river like the Thames and as formidable, as spectacular and as bustling as this bridge in London'. Paul Hentzner, a German visitor, writing in 1598, described the structure:

> On the south is a bridge of stone, eight hundred feet in length, of wonderful work; it is supported upon twenty piers of square stone, sixty feet high and thirty broad, joined by arches of about twenty feet diameter. The whole is covered on each side with houses so disposed as to have the appearance of a continued street, not at all of a bridge.

Thomas Platter commented that there were 'many tall, handsome merchant dwellings, and expensive shops, where all manner of wares are for sale resembling a long street'.

It is truly a remarkable bridge, the first river crossing upstream from the mouth of the Thames and the longest inhabited bridge ever built. It does have some Continental rivals, notably the Ponte Vecchio in Florence (1345) and the much more modern Rialto in Venice which was opened in 1591 and, unlike London and Florence, is a single-arch construction.

The earliest known bridge across the Thames in London was probably built about 1500 BC at Vauxhall, a few miles west of the current bridge. In those days the Thames was much wider and shallower and the bridge may have been one of a series joining a chain of islands across the stream. The first bridge in the centre of London was built in Roman times to allow the Roman army to move quickly from the Kent coast, across the Thames to deal with any trouble. After the Roman period, bridges were built by the Saxons. William the Conqueror constructed a new one, but this was destroyed by the London tornado of 1091 and his son had to rebuild it. Following a fire, a new wooden bridge was built in 1163. In 1176, during the reign of Henry II, Peter de Colechurch, Chaplain of St Mary Colechurch, began to build a stone structure. Work on the bridge started six years after the murder of St Thomas à Becket in Canterbury cathedral and it became the official starting point for pilgrims going from London to pray at Becket's shrine in Canterbury. The bridge was built by driving wooden piles into the river bed at low tide to form a rectangle. The resulting space was filled with rubble and then Kentish rag stones were added to form the arches. It is sometimes said that London Bridge is built on wool – this is because Henry II imposed taxes on wool, undressed sheepskins and leather to pay for the construction. Peter de Colechurch died in 1205 and did not live to see the completion of the structure, which was not finished until 1209. King John leased out building plots on the bridge for shops and houses to raise money to cover the costs of the work.

The bridge consists of nineteen arches and is very narrow, the roadway across being only 12ft (4m) wide, about the same width as the nearby Fish Street Hill. It is so narrow that two carriages can scarcely pass one another and getting across can take up to an hour. Towards the centre of the bridge is a drawbridge to allow boats to pass through or, as we shall see, to prevent access to the City during times of trouble. The houses and shops along its sides are very remarkable and well worth a visit. At the south end is the Great Stone Gate and beyond that is the building known as the 'house of many windows', a comparatively modern structure. Further along, near the drawbridge, is Nonsuch House. This was built in 1577 and is a large four-storey building with turrets surmounted by cupolas and large bay windows overlooking the river. It is the home to wealthy City merchants – mercers and haberdashers.

As Thomas Platter said, it is full of wealthy shops. There are haberdashers who sell ribbons, beads, gloves and other small items, others who sell hats, there are also milliners, a shoemaker, hosiers, silkmen, glovers, linen drapers, woollen drapers and grocers.

Peter de Colechurch built a chapel dedicated to St Thomas à Becket in the middle of the bridge. Becket and Peter had probably known each other because Becket was born in the parish of St Mary Colechurch. The chapel was a two-storey structure which projected out beyond the line of the bridge. It was very much a pilgrims' chapel for those going to Canterbury, but it also served watermen and fishermen who had their own entrance at river level. After his death, Peter's body was interred in the chapel. In 1387, it was rebuilt in the Perpendicular style with pointed arches and stained glass windows. It continued to serve pilgrims and watermen until Henry VIII's break with Rome. In 1538, the Pope ordered a crusade against England and the dedication of the chapel was quickly changed from St Thomas à Becket to St Thomas the Apostle. The number of priests was reduced and a painter was employed to deface and change the images of Becket and an embroiderer was hired to rework the representation of the saint into that of Our Lady. In 1548, the chapel was closed, and subsequently turned into a house and shop and leased to a grocer, William Bridger.

Because London Bridge is the entrance to London from Kent and also from the Continent, it has witnessed some of the most triumphal and tragic events in England's history. The first significant event occurred in 1212, three years after construction had finished. A major fire, sometimes known as the Great Fire of Southwark, started south of the river. The Church of St Mary Overie was badly damaged and the flames spread to the houses at the south end of the bridge. A crowd of people rushed on to the bridge from the north, either to help extinguish the flames, or just to gawp. Then the wind blew hot embers across the bridge, igniting the houses at the north end. The people in the middle were trapped. Boats were sent to rescue them, 'into which the multitude so inadvisedly rushed that the ships being drowned, they all perished', John Stow, *Survey of London*. Estimates put the death toll at 30,000, but this is almost certainly an exaggeration.

The next drama occurred in 1263 during the revolt by Simon de Montfort and some of the barons against Henry III. London joined in the uprising leaving Henry and his hated queen, Eleanor of Provence, trapped in the Tower. Eleanor tried to escape by boat to join her son (the future Edward I) at Windsor, but the Londoners pelted her with eggs, stones, mud, vegetables and pieces of paving and she had to be rescued by the Lord Mayor and taken to the Bishop of London's residence.

Perhaps the most extraordinary event to have taken place on the bridge was the joust on St George's Day, 1390 between Lord John Welles, the English ambassador to Scotland, and Sir David de Lindesay, Earl of Crawford. The story began when Welles was at a banquet, where he argued with his Scottish hosts as to whether the English or the Scots were more courageous. He then offered to joust with any Scotsman at any time or any place. He turned to Lindesay and challenged him directly, saying that he had been more boastful than the rest of the Scots. Welles was allowed to choose the location for the joust and selected London Bridge on St George's Day since St George had been a warrior.

Lindesay rode down to London with thirty-two of his supporters. On the day, a great crowd of nobles and ordinary people had gathered and King Richard II was there to witness the spectacle. The bridge was decked out with flags and covered with soil to enable the horses to gallop. At the first charge, both spurred their horses and raced together with great force, their lances at the ready. Neither was unseated, and their lances were shattered. The crowd, which supported the local boy, claimed that Lindesay was cheating because he had tied himself to his saddle and that was why he had not been unseated. To prove them wrong, Lindesay immediately leapt down from his horse and then, although he was wearing heavy armour, he jumped back upon it without any assistance. Taking another lance, he entered the lists once more, and again it was shattered. Then they collided a third time, this time using sturdier lances. At this point, the English challenger was unhorsed and fell on the ground with a great crash, unconscious. A huge groan went up from the English spectators. Lindesay was victorious, but he was a true knight and he quickly dismounted and ran to his opponent to tend him until the physicians arrived and he recovered consciousness. Then he did not let a single day go by without paying a visit to the injured Welles, and he addressed him in a kindly manner, as if he were his dearest friend. He remained in England for three months and was treated with the greatest honour.

But, like all disputes between England and Scotland, the losing side could not let it go. There was a big dispute between the followers of Welles and the followers of Lindesay and an English courtier challenged a Highlander called David to a sword fight without armour. It was agreed that the fight would take place in a market place in London and that neither man would leave until the victor had been decided. But, according to the (Scottish) chronicler, when the English courtier arrived and saw the Scot ready for the fight he feared for his life and called it off. Lindesay eventually returned to Scotland and, believing that he had won the fight as a result of the divine intercession of St George, he gave lands to fund a college of seven priests at Dundee who would worship St George by singing perpetual hymns to the Virgin. Still the English would not give up and the next year, the Englishman Sir Robert Morley arrived in Scotland, challenging any comer to a joust. Archibald Adamston fought him and was defeated, and then Hugh Wallace had the same misfortune. The Englishman competed for a third time against Thomas Trail at Berwick and was unhorsed by his adversary. Many other jousts were fought by noblemen of both countries with varying results, some in England and others in Scotland.

King Henry V was another whose journeys over the bridge marked major stages in his life. In 1415, he returned to London, the triumphant victor of the Battle of Agincourt. He was met to the south of London by a huge crowd of nobles and citizens, as well as representatives of the livery companies wearing red cloaks with hoods of black fur. A mile from the City, he was greeted by many clergy wearing rich copes and carrying censers. The bridge was decked out splendidly for his arrival. At the gate at the south of the bridge he was met by male and female giants, the male one carrying a large spear and a mighty axe. At the drawbridge there were the goddesses of nature, grace and fortune wearing golden crowns and seven attendant maidens also wearing crowns. There were trumpeters in the turrets and a tower built across the bridge with the effigy of St George, his head adorned with laurels interwoven with jewels. At the drawbridge gate there were two outworks, one supporting a lion holding a lance and the other an antelope from whose neck hung a shield bearing the royal arms.

Henry had a second triumphant entry across the bridge in 1420 when he returned with his new bride, Catherine de Valois, the daughter of King Charles VI of France. Two years later, however, he died of dysentery while on military campaign in France, never having seen his young son, the future Henry VI. His body was returned to London and was met in Southwark by the mayor and aldermen wearing white robes, while 500 men of arms in black harness accompanied the procession carrying their spears reversed, while 300 others carried long torches. As the funeral carriage crossed the bridge, fifteen splendidly dressed bishops chanted the Office for the Dead.

In 1522, Charles V, the Holy Roman Emperor and the most powerful ruler in the West whose territories stretched from the Channel to the Baltic and the Adriatic, paid a visit to London. His route passed through Southwark and he was greeted by the mayor and officers of the City as well as the Chancellor, Sir Thomas More, who made a speech of welcome. The bridge was decorated to celebrate his arrival and included two giants, Hercules holding a club and Sampson the jaw bone of an ass. Further down the bridge was a building made to look like a black and white castle; above this was a scene showing Jason with a golden fleece. On one side was a dragon and on the other two bulls continuously spewing fire.

One of the most famous and gruesome sights on the bridge are the heads of traitors which are placed on the gate building at the south end of the bridge. The practice began in 1305 when William Wallace, one of the leaders of the Scottish wars of independence, was executed at Smithfield and his head was dipped in tar and impaled on a long spike. The Tudors were particularly keen on executing traitors; foreign visitors counted large number of heads there, in 1592 Jacob Rathgeb saw thirty-four heads, while in 1602 the Duke of Stettin saw thirty.

The symbolism of placing a head on the bridge was hugely important and this was realised by rebels as well as the rulers. During the Peasants' Revolt of 1381, the Archbishop of Canterbury and the Lord Treasurer,

Robert Hales, together with two other courtiers were seized and beheaded when the rebels captured the Tower of London. The archbishop's head, wearing his mitre, was put on a pole and placed on the bridge. Two days later, Wat Tyler, the leader of the revolt, was killed by the Mayor of London and the authorities regained control of the City. Tyler's head replaced that of the archbishop.

The only major battle on the bridge occurred in 1450 when the government was threatened by a serious rebellion headed by Jack Cade. He brought an army of 5,000 rebels from Kent and occupied Southwark. On 3 July, they crossed the bridge and seized and executed Lord Saye and Sele, one of the king's hated advisors and a rapacious landlord; they also killed his son-in-law, William Cromer. The heads of Lord Saye and Sele and Cromer were paraded round London on poles and made to kiss one another, then placed on London Bridge. According to Shakespeare, Cade urged his followers on saying, 'but first go and set London Bridge on fire, and, if you can, burn down the Tower too.... Now go some and pull down the Savoy. Others to th' Inns of Court. Down with them all!' (*Henry VI, Part I*).

The rebels behaved so badly that the Londoners, who had originally been sympathetic, turned against them and sought the help of Captain Matthew Gough, a Welsh veteran of the wars in France, and Lord Scales, another veteran, who were both stationed in the Tower of London. When the rebels returned to Southwark for the night a force of Londoners led by Gough seized the bridge. The rebels counter-attacked and set fire to the properties on the bridge, many of the inhabitants died as a result of the fire or through drowning. A battle raged across the bridge all night and Gough was killed. Eventually, at 8am a truce was called and Cade fled with a large amount of booty. He was tracked down by Alexander Iden, the Sheriff of Kent. Iden and his companions wounded Cade so badly that he died on his way to London. Nonetheless, his body was duly beheaded and his head replaced those of his victims on the bridge.

Putting a head on the gate sometimes had the opposite effect to that which was intended. On 17 June 1535, John Fisher, the Bishop of Rochester, was tried for treason before a court in Westminster Hall because he had denied that Henry VIII was supreme head of the Church.

The court included Thomas Cromwell and Anne Boleyn's father – Fisher had been a supporter of her predecessor, Catherine of Aragon. He was executed at Tower Hill on 22 June and his head placed on the bridge. But then things began to go wrong – his head showed no signs of decay but 'daily grew fresher and fresher so that in his life he never looked so well'. The head became a place of pilgrimage for many thousands and after a fortnight it had to be taken down at night and thrown in the river.

Thomas More, Henry VIII's former Chancellor, was executed on 6 July 1535 for refusing to accept Henry VIII as supreme head of the Church and his head too was placed on London Bridge. There are a number of stories about its fate. One story is that More's head did not decay, a missing tooth regrew and his grey hair became reddish or yellow. Another is that his daughter, Margaret Roper, was travelling under the bridge and looked at his head, saying 'that head which has layn many a time in my lap, would to God it would fall into my lap as I pass under' and, so the story goes, it did. It seems likely that Margaret bribed the Keeper of Heads on the bridge to sell her More's head which was buried with her in a lead box when she died. Thomas Cromwell was executed in 1540 and his head placed on the bridge.

In 1560, the heads were put to another use. The Royal Mint had brought over some Dutch and German workers to help melt down old coins as part of a scheme to produce a new coinage. One stage of the process involved the use of arsenic and the fumes began to make the workers ill. There was a popular belief that drinking from a skull was a cure for arsenic poisoning and the skulls from the bridge were used for this purpose. Sadly, it did not work and most of the workmen died.

Although many of the stories of the Bridge are of rebellion and executions, at least one man's fortune was made by it. Edward Osborne was an apprentice to William Hewitt, a wealthy clothworker who lived with his family and his apprentice on London Bridge. One day, Hewitt's daughter, Anne, was playing with a maid near a window and leaned out and fell into the water. Osborne jumped in and saved her. The family later moved to Philpot Lane and Osborne went with them. Because of his wealth and position (he became Lord Mayor in 1559), Hewitt's daughter was an attractive catch for several young men, but he encouraged the brave Osborne to marry her, saying, 'No, Osborne saved her and Osborne shall marry her'. Osborne inherited much of his father-in-law's property, including estates in Yorkshire. He was also a successful merchant, trading with Turkey and the East and became governor of the Levant Company and was Lord Mayor in 1583. His great-grandson became the first Duke of Leeds in 1694.

The bridge is a major obstacle across the river and makes navigation difficult, particularly at times of low tide. Things were made worse in 1437 when the Great Stone Gate at the south end of the bridge collapsed into the stream partially blocking one of the arches and the masonry was never removed. In the 1580s a water mill was erected on the north side to pump water out of the river to supply people's houses while corn mills were built on the south side of the bridge in the 1590s. This has further restricted the flow of the river and made it much more angry, difficult and dangerous to navigate when it flows under the bridge, particularly when the tide is flowing out.

The Tower

John Stow, the Elizabethan writer on London, described the functions of the Tower of London:

> This Tower is a citadel to defend or command the city; a royal palace for assemblies or treaties; a prison of state for the most dangerous offendors; the only place of coinage for all England at this time; the armoury for warlike provisions; the treasury of the ornaments and jewels of the crown and general conservator of the most records of the king's courts of justice at Westminster.

Stow, who was a serious minded man, failed to add that the Tower was also a zoo for wild animals.

Opening Hours

Opens:	Sunrise
Closes for dinner:	11am
Reopens:	1pm
Closes:	5pm

Drawbridges reopen briefly at 8pm to allow visitors to leave and residents who have been out in the City to return home.

What to See

There are a lot of things to be seen at the Tower. These include a collection of arms and armour – artillery, bows and arrows and crossbows. There are also many fine furnishings from when the Tower was a royal residence – gilt bedsteads, curtains, tapestries, table-covers and cushions in gold and silver. It is also possible to visit the Mint and the Zoo. People enjoy seeing where the executions of nobles are carried out. The main benefit of visiting the Tower, however, is a chance to understand its place in the history of London and the country.

Admission Charges

It is a very expensive place to visit. When Thomas Platter came, he had to pay tips to guides in every area he went in. In the end he paid eight separate tips to different officials. This cost him £1 and 4s., equivalent to about twelve weeks' work for a poor labourer.

The Zoo

There has been a zoo in the Tower since 1235 when the Holy Roman Emperor sent Henry III (his brother-in-law) three leopards. These died but a lion arrived in 1240 and in 1251 Henry moved the royal collection of animals from Woodstock to the Tower. In 1252, he was given a polar bear by King Haakon IV of Norway. This animal was sometimes tied to a long strong cord and allowed to swim and catch fish in the Thames. In 1255, Louis IX of France sent an elephant, which arrived at the Tower on a large river boat. Unfortunately, it died two years later and its bones were given to Westminster abbey to be carved into boxes to house the bones, hair, teeth, etc. of saints. Edward I built a Lion Tower where the animals were housed. Richard II was given a camel in 1392, while his wife, Anne of Bohemia, was given a pelican, a sign of piety. In 1445, Henry VI married Margaret of Anjou whose father Rene, despite his poverty (he is mocked as Regnier, a poor king in Shakespeare's *Henry VI, Part I*), was a mad keen animal collector and had the largest menagerie of the fifteenth century. He converted the moat of his castle at Angers into a zoo and had a collection that included tigers, lions, leopards, wolves, stags, camels, wild goats, elephants, boars and a variety of exotic birds. He gave the happy couple a lion for a wedding gift.

More recent monarchs have continued the tradition of keeping a zoo. In 1578, at the Tower Grenade saw six or seven lions and lionesses, a leopard 'excellently spotted', a porcupine and a wolf. In 1592, when Joseph Rathgeb, secretary of Frederick Duke of Wurtemberg, visited the Tower he wrote, 'In this Tower also, but in separate small houses made of wood, are kept six lions and lionesses … not far from there is also a lean, ugly wolf, which is the only one in England, on this account it is kept by the Queen'. When Hentzner visited the Tower in 1596, he was shown three lionesses, a large lion called Edward VI, a tiger, a lynx, a very old wolf, a porcupine and an eagle.

James I has a rather different view of animals and has built an exercise yard with a great platform where he can sit and enjoy the spectacle of animals fighting. In 1610, he arranged a fight between three mastiffs and a lion. Two of the dogs were killed and a third was injured but its life was spared because of the intervention of the king's son, Prince Henry, who declared: 'He had fought the king of the wild animals and should never again have to fight baser creatures!'

The Mint

The Mint was set up in the Tower in 1279 at the west end between the inner and outer curtain walls. It produces about £30,000 of coins a month and is open to visitors. The process is very complex and involves a lot of heat and hammering. Gold is cast into ingots which have to be hammered into thin blanks and annealed (heated and then allowed to cool slowly) to harden the metal. Then blanks are then cleaned and placed between a pair of hand-held dies. The pile, or lower die, has a spiked end to enable it to be driven firmly into a block of wood; a blank is placed on top of the pile and above it is held the trussel or upper die. The trussel is then struck a blow with a hammer, causing the blank to be impressed with the obverse and reverse design.

The Artillery

The Tower is the home of a formidable collection of artillery. According to Grenade, every battlement and loophole has a piece of artillery with its carriage, while other cannon are placed in front of the Tower. Every Thursday, the gunners from the Tower go to a piece of open land off Bishopsgate and fire their guns into an earthwork butt. Part of the Tower is used for making guns and for storing weapons. According to Grenade, it had enough to equip 50,000 men with pikes, arquebuses (guns) and corselets (armour for the torso). This has attracted gunsmiths and armourers to set up shop in the local streets; there is a gun foundry in Houndsditch. So, if you are in the market for armour or weapons, this is the place to go.

Ceremonial

The Tower plays its part in the ceremonies of the country. New ambassadors coming to London alight at the Tower where they are greeted with a salute of gunfire and then escorted through the City by dignitaries. Until the reign of Queen Elizabeth, monarchs would spend the night before their coronation in the Tower, but King James has not followed this tradition. Henry IV's coronation was particularly magnificent because, having usurped the Crown from Richard II, he needed to put on a good show. So, by a miracle, some oil that had been given by the Virgin Mary to St Thomas à Becket had been found in the cellars of the Tower, where it had laid undiscovered for centuries, and this was used to anoint the new king. He began the tradition of creating Knights of the Bath at his coronation, which took place in October, a chilly time of the year.

A total of forty-six squires were chosen and forty-six baths were placed in the Tower, each with its own canopy. Each candidate bathed, and the king made a speech and made the sign of the cross on their back. They then dried, dressed in monks' robes and spent the night in prayer and meditation. The next day, dressed in new armour, the king created them as knights and presented each of them with a long green cloak lined with white ermine. Then Henry and his entourage of 6,000 nobles and grandees and their followers on horseback set off for Westminster. During the ride he passed nine fountains flowing with red and white wine – a good thing to do if you want to win the support of Londoners.

History

There is a widespread and erroneous belief that the Tower was built by Julius Caesar. When Thomas Platter visited in 1599 he was shown a large hall in which Julius Caesar dined and a tower that Caesar had had constucted. When Grenade wrote his account of London in 1578 he also claimed that Caesar had built the Tower. In *Richard II* by Shakespeare, the queen says, 'This is the way the king will come. This is the way to Julius Caesar's ill-erected tower.'

Work on the Tower started soon after William the Conqueror had invaded England. He had laid waste to the area round London and eventually the Londoners surrendered, but he needed to maintain control over the City, so he employed Gundulf, the new Bishop of Rochester, to manage the project to build a tower that would overawe them. His first structure to be built was the White Tower. Norman masons were used and some of the building stone was specially imported from Caen in Normandy, while other stone came from Kent. Labour, however, was provided by Englishmen. The Anglo-Saxon Chronicle comments in 1097 that 'many shires whose labour was due to London were hard pressed because of the wall that they built around the Tower'.

William never saw the White Tower completed as it was not finished until 1100 during the reign of his son, William Rufus. Nothing like it had been seen in London, it was immense, 27.5m high and 36m x 32.5m across. It dominated the London skyline. It was protected by Roman walls on two sides, ditches to the north and west and an earthwork surmounted by a wooden palisade. The walls were enormously thick, 5m at the base and 3.3m at the top. Henry III undertook huge developments at the Tower to make it into a palace as well as a fortress. The moat was widened by a Flemish expert, Master John, and new walls and towers were constructed. The Wakefield Tower was built by Henry III as the king's private quarters with its own Watergate and he began the tradition of whitewashing the White Tower which gave it its name. Edward I undertook further work on the Tower, filling in Henry's moat and erecting a new curtain wall. A new moat was dug outside the new wall, a new entrance was provided and a new Watergate (later known as Traitor's Gate) was added. Much of the form of the Tower as it survives today was the responsibility of Edward I.

Henry VIII added the Tudor buildings used to accommodate the senior staff of the Tower and the cupolas on the tops of the White Tower. He also rebuilt the Tower's own church, St Peter ad Vincula, after an earlier church on the site had burned down. The dedication of the church 'St Peter in Chains' comes from the story of how the apostle Peter was imprisoned by King Herod, but the night before his trial an angel came to rescue him. It is most famous as the place of burial for many people who were executed by Henry VIII, including Anne Boleyn, Catherine Howard, Thomas Cromwell, Thomas More and John Fisher. None were given a memorial and the main monuments in the church are to officials of the Tower.

Prisoners

The Tower has obtained its sinister reputation as a prison for important people, most of whom took a one-way trip through Traitor's Gate. The use of the Tower for this purpose became more common in the late fifteenth century, when the Duke of Clarence, brother of Edward IV, was tried for plotting to overthrow the king. There are serious doubts about Clarence's mental state – he had defended one of his retainers who had used necromancy to secure the king's death. He had also abducted Ankarette Twynho from Somerset in April 1477 and had her indicted, convicted and executed in a single day on false charges of poisoning his wife. Clarence was tried in 1478 and sentenced to death. According to some stories, he was given his own choice of how this was to be carried out and he decided to be drowned in a butt or barrel of malmsey (sweet wine from Greece). This story is told by chroniclers and is taken seriously by some historians.

It was the Tudors who really gave the Tower its reputation as a place of horror, imprisonment and death. Henry VIII had two of his wives, Anne Boleyn and Catherine Howard, imprisoned and executed there, as well as his ministers, Thomas More and Thomas Cromwell. Perhaps the outstanding act of brutality of his reign was the execution of Margaret Pole, Countess of Salisbury, in 1541. She was the daughter of the Duke of Clarence who had also died in the Tower and her real offence was to be the mother of Cardinal Pole, a supporter of Catherine of Aragon and the Pope's agent in stirring up trouble against Henry in other European countries. Margaret was a difficult person – she had been governess to Henry's daughter, Mary, but had refused to hand over Mary's jewels to Henry. Nevertheless, she was 68 at the time of her execution and no real threat to anyone.

Like her mother, Anne Boleyn, Queen Elizabeth was imprisoned in the Tower by her sister, Mary. Elizabeth was made of tough stuff and when she arrived at Traitor's Gate she refused to get out of the boat and then sat down on the steps and would not enter the Tower. Eventually, she was persuaded to go inside where she was shown to the same set of rooms that her mother had occupied before her execution. Elizabeth was constantly questioned while in the Tower and was accused of involvement in Wyatt's Rebellion. Luckily, her sister relented and she was released (but kept in a form of house arrest) after two-and-a-half months.

Queen Elizabeth has also made use of the Tower as a prison and place of execution. The Duke of Norfolk, who was involved in a conspiracy to marry Mary, Queen of Scots, depose Elizabeth and restore Catholicism, was imprisoned and executed there in 1572. The Earl of Essex was executed there in 1601 following a rebellion against the queen.

The strangest current inhabitant of the Tower is Sir Walter Raleigh. He is a soldier, writer, courtier and explorer. He fought in the wars in

Ireland, funded and arranged expeditions to Virginia, explored in central and south America, and was involved in naval attacks on Spain. In 1591, he was secretly married to Elizabeth Throckmorton. She was one of the queen's ladies in waiting and was pregnant at the time. She gave birth to a son, believed to be named Damerei, who died in October 1592. Bess resumed her duties to the queen. The following year, the unauthorised marriage was discovered and the queen ordered Raleigh imprisoned and Bess dismissed from court. Both were imprisoned in the Tower in June 1592. They were eventually released, but Raleigh fell foul of King James, being accused of treason for his part in a plot led by Lord Cobham to overthrow the king and replace him with his cousin, Lady Arbella Stuart, and he has been imprisoned in the Tower for many years under sentence of death.

Since his imprisonment, Raleigh has made good use of his time. He has written tracts, pamphlets and the first part of *A History of the World*. He has set up a herb garden and makes various potions, including his famous Great Cordial made from plants from the Amazon. He has been visited by many people including the queen, Anne of Denmark, and has struck up a friendship with Prince Henry, the heir to the throne. Since 1605 he has had congenial company because the Earl of Northumberland has also been imprisoned. Northumberland is known as 'the wizard Earl' because of his interest in science and his large library. He has set up his own laboratory in the Tower and regularly discusses scientific ideas with Raleigh.

Escapes

Although the Tower looks impregnable and must have dispirited most of those who were imprisoned there, a few brave souls managed to escape – this was a very small number indeed, roughly one every twenty-five years.

Ranulph Flambard was the first prisoner in the Tower and also the first escapee. He had been the Chief Minister to William Rufus and had taken part in that king's extortionate efforts to increase revenues. He was also responsible for the start of construction work on London Bridge and, ironically, built a wall round the White Tower in London. When William died childless in 1100, his brother Henry, the new king, imprisoned Ranulph in the Tower on a charge of embezzlement. Ranulph's friends sent him a rope in a flagon of wine. He gave the wine to his gaolers and when they were drunk and asleep, he climbed out of the window of his cell and down the rope. His friends had arranged for a ship to be waiting to take him, some of his treasure and his elderly mother to France and freedom. The Constable of the Tower at the time, William de Mandeville, was punished, losing his job and a third of his estates.

Gruffydd ap Llywelyn was the son of Llywelyn the Great, the ruler of Wales. Although Gruffydd was the older son, his father favoured his younger son Dafydd. When Llywelyn died, Gruffydd was captured by his brother and following a successful invasion of the Welsh borders by the English, he and his son Owain were handed over to Henry III in 1241 as a hostage for the good behaviour of the Welsh. Despite his wife paying a ransom, Henry III kept them both in the Tower. On St David's Day, 1244, Gruffydd made a rope from sheets and clothes and tried to climb down from the Tower. Sadly, he was a tall and heavy man, the rope broke and he fell to his death

In 1321, Roger Mortimer, Earl of March, led a revolt against the unpopular King Edward II. However, he was captured and in July 1322, he and his uncle (also called Roger) were tried and condemned to death, but on 22 July their sentence was commuted to one of perpetual imprisonment. Roger Mortimer and his uncle were kept in close and uncomfortable custody in the Tower. On 1 August 1323 (the feast of St Peter in Chains), with the connivance of Gerard de Alspaye, who had custody of him, and after the guards (and Stephen Seagrave, the constable) had been drugged, Roger Mortimer escaped. He crossed the Thames in a boat that awaited him, rode to Dover and, in spite of strenuous efforts to recapture him, succeeded in crossing to France. He was welcomed in Paris by Charles IV, then at war with Edward II.

The most famous escape and a very recent one, was that by John Gerard, a Jesuit who had been secretly offering support to Catholics in England. He was arrested in 1594 and taken to the Tower where he was tortured in order to force him to reveal the whereabouts of Father Henry

Garnet, another priest who was hiding in London. He described how he was tortured in his autobiography:

> Then they led me to a great upright beam or pillar of wood which was one of the supports of this vast crypt. At the summit of this column were fixed certain iron staples for supporting weights. Here they placed on my wrists gauntlets of iron, and ordered me to mount upon two or three wicker steps; then raising my arms, they inserted an iron bar through the rings of the gauntlets and then through the staples in the pillar, putting a pin through the bar so that it could not slip. My arms being thus fixed above my head, they withdrew those wicker steps I spoke of, one by one, from beneath my feet, so that I hung by my hands and arms.

Despite the intense pain, Gerard kept silent and after three torture sessions the authorities gave up. He was kept prisoner in the Salt Tower but he managed to communicate with his friends outside by sending them rosaries he had made out of orange peel wrapped in paper. He wrote his messages on the paper using orange juice which his friends were able to read by holding the paper up to a fire. They would reply by sending him sweetmeats also wrapped in paper with secret messages written in orange juice. After a time, he realised that his gaoler who was carrying the secret messages could not read and so he began to write more openly using a pencil.

In 1597, while still in the Salt Tower, Gerard made the acquaintance of another Catholic, John Arden, who had been in prison for many years and was lucky enough to have a cell that gave him access to the roof which overlooked the moat. He eventually persuaded the gaoler to allow him to dine with Arden in his cell and spend the night there. Then he hatched his daring escape plan. At first, he and Arden tried bribing the gaoler, but he resolutely refused to help. Instead, Gerard decided to get hold of a rope and use it to climb down from the Tower and across the moat to freedom.

His first attempt failed miserably. The plan was for him to throw a lead weight attached to a piece of string out from the Tower to where his friends were waiting. They would then attach the end of this string to a strong rope which Gerard and Arden would pull back up the Tower, fasten it tight and make their escape. The friends arrived by boat but were spotted by a man who lived close to the Tower and had to wait until he had gone to bed. Unfortunately, they waited so long that they had to abandon the mission. As they were rowing away, their boat was caught by the rising tide and dashed against London Bridge. They only escaped because of a brave rescue effort by another boat, while one of them managed to grab hold of a rope that had been let down from the bridge and was pulled to safety.

The next night they tried again and managed to get the rope up to their tower and looped round a large canon. Arden, who was a strong man, climbed down, but Gerard, whose arms and hands had been badly weakened by torture, struggled to get down the rope and eventually got stuck on the wall next to the moat. Luckily, one of his companions climbed up the wall and managed to bring him down. Although unable to walk because of his exertions, he was helped into the boat and to freedom.

Chapter Four

Other Attractions

As well as the must-see sights, London has a large number of other interesting places to visit – churches, palaces and other historical tourist attractions.

The Eleanor Crosses

In 1290, Eleanor of Castile, wife of Edward I, died at Harby, near Lincoln. Her embalmed body was carried to Westminster abbey for burial. The funeral procession rested at different towns every night and Edward subsequently ordered that crosses be erected at the places where his wife's body had lain. London has two of the crosses. One in Cheapside and the other at the junction of Whitehall, Cockspur Street and The Strand which is known as Charing Cross. The Londoners will tell you that the name Charing comes from the French *chère reine*, but the name predates the cross and probably comes from the Anglo–Saxon 'cerring' meaning a bend, because the river bends at that point. According to Grenade, many Londoners were ignorant of the origins of the cross, 'some say that it is the work of Romans from the time when Julius Caesar occupied England. Others conjecture that it was Queen Eleanor, the wife of King Edward the first of that name.' It is octagonal, very tall and probably higher than Westminster abbey and is made of ashlar stone and marble. Unfortunately, it is very weather-beaten now.

The cross in Cheapside is taller than the neighbouring churches and is probably about 125ft high. It was rebuilt between 1484 and 1486. It was regilded in 1533 for the coronation of Anne Boleyn and again in 1554 in preparation for the possible visit of King Philip of Spain. It is very unpopular with some of the more puritanical Londoners who object to the religious sculptures. In 1581, it was vandalised and the Christian images – the Virgin Mary, Edward the Confessor and Christ's Resurrection – were broken and defaced but it was later repaired. In 1599, the timber under the lead at the top of the memorial was found to be rotten and was removed. The monument remained in a state of disrepair until the Privy Council wrote to the Lord Mayor on behalf of the queen insisting that it be repaired, which was done. However, twelve days after the work was finished, it was again vandalised. It is also much disliked by some local residents who claim it holds up the traffic. In view of this opposition, it would be worth seeing while it is still in existence.

Bridewell Palace

The exterior of this building is very magnificent, but you may not wish to visit the interior. It is located at the junction of the River Thames and the River Fleet near the eastern end of Fleet Street. It takes its name from a spring near to St Bride's Church. The palace was built by Henry VIII between 1515 and 1523 because he was short of accommodation after a disastrous fire at the Palace of Westminster in 1512. It was used to accommodate the entourage of Charles V, the Holy Roman Emperor, who visited London in 1522. Charles himself stayed across the River Fleet in Blackfriars Monastery and a bridge was built across the Fleet to link the two buildings. Six years later, Henry and Catherine of Aragon stayed there while the papal legates deliberated on their divorce proceedings. Most of Act III of Shakespeare's *Henry VIII* which concerns those events is set in Bridewell. The palace was used intermittently by the king until 1530 when the fall of Thomas Wolsey allowed him to acquire Wolsey's Whitehall Palace.

For a time it was given to favoured ambassadors as a residence. Hans Holbein may have painted his famous picture *The Ambassadors* there. Edward VI gave the palace to the City of London in 1553 as an orphanage and a house of correction for, as described by Grenade, 'idlers, vagabonds, whoremongers, harlots, and such similar lazy scoundrels so that they might be taught to earn their bread by the sweat of their brows'. Other towns have begun to set up houses of correction and the name Bridewell is coming to be used as a term for a workhouse for the idle and unemployed.

The Guildhall

The building was started in 1411 and finished in 1440 and lies on the site of a Roman amphitheatre, parts of which may have survived until the thirteenth century. The building itself is large and prestigious, and Grenade described it as being 'like a truly great and magnificent palace'. Inside the hall are effigies of the famous armed giants Gogmagog and Corineus.

It is the centre of the City of London' administration, the meeting place for the Courts of Aldermen and Common Council. Although the main court for hearing criminal trials in London is the Justice Hall next to Newgate Prison in Old Bailey, the Guildhall is also sometimes used for major trials for treason and piracy. Lady Jane Grey was tried there, as were two of the lovers of Queen Catherine Howard and Henry Garnet, the Gunpowder Plot conspirator. In 1594, Rodrigo Lopez, a Portuguese Jew who had converted to Christianity and is sometime said to be the model for Shakespeare's *The Merchant of Venice*, was tried there for conspiring to poison the queen.

The Charterhouse

Like many buildings, the Charterhouse was originally a monastery. It is located near Smithfield at the corner of Charterhouse Square. It has been in the hands of the Howard family – with some interruptions – between 1565 and 1611. Thomas Howard, the fourth Duke of Norfolk, owned the property and he spent lavishly to improve it, but in 1571 he was arrested for his part in a plot to replace Queen Elizabeth with Mary, Queen of Scots. He spent a period under house arrest in the Charterhouse and occupied his time by doing building works, including installing a tennis court. He was executed in 1572. His eldest son, Philip Howard, later the Earl of Arundel, then inherited the property and let it out to various people including the Portuguese ambassador. In 1589, Philip Howard was condemned to death for treason (he had been corresponding with Mary, Queen of Scots) and, although the sentence was commuted to life imprisonment, he lost his property. In 1601, the queen granted it to Philip's half-brother Lord Thomas Howard. He constructed a great staircase and did other works, but his main interest was the magnificent new house he was building at Audley End and in 1611 he sold the Charterhouse to Thomas Sutton for £11,000.

Sutton was the richest commoner in England, and had been a coal mine owner and money lender. His plan was to set up a charity at the Charterhouse for eighty elderly men and a school for forty boys. The brothers had to be over 50, of good behaviour and soundness in religion and there was a preference for those who had been servants to the king, decrepit or old captains at sea or land, maimed or disabled soldiers, merchants fallen on hard times, those ruined by shipwreck or other calamity or held prisoner by the Turks. The boys simply had to be sons of poor parents. Sutton did not live to see his school and hospital set up – he died soon after he had acquired the property, but his executors managed to complete the necessary building works and the school and almshouse were launched in 1614.

Westminster Abbey

As well as St Paul's Cathedral, the great church of Westminster abbey is well worth seeing. It was originally a Benedictine monastery founded under the patronage of King Edgar and Saint Dunstan. King Edward the Confessor built a church there dedicated to St Peter the Apostle. It became known as the west minster, as opposed to St Paul's Cathedral which was the east minster being situated a mile and a half to the north east. Edward was buried in the church and in the 1240s, Henry III decided to rebuild it in the Gothic style and to provide an elaborate tomb for the Confessor. Every English king and queen since William the Conqueror has been crowned there (except Edward V who was not crowned) and many are buried there. Henry VII replaced Henry III's chapel dedicated to the Virgin Mary with a Lady Chapel in the Perpendicular Gothic style. It is probably the most magnificent building in England. It was used for the burial of Henry and some of his successors – Edward VI, Queen Mary and Queen Elizabeth. Mary, Queen of Scots was also buried there; she had originally been interred in Peterborough cathedral, but her son King James had her remains removed and reburied in a tomb in the Abbey.

The Benedictine abbey was abolished by Henry VIII who made the church into a cathedral with its own bishop. The bishop was removed by Edward VI and the abbey became a cathedral within the London diocese. Queen Mary restored the Benedictine abbey with an abbot and monks. On Queen Elizabeth's accession, the abbey was again abolished and the church became a collegiate church and a royal peculiar, exempt from the jurisdiction of bishops.

Adjacent to the abbey are the Jewel Tower, a fourteenth-century survival from the palace of Westminster, and Westminster Hall, a magnificent building with its huge wooden hammer beam roof and now used for the main law courts. Shakespeare sets some dramatic scenes there – the deposition of Richard II and the trial of the Duke of Buckingham in *Henry VIII*.

Churches

London has a huge number of churches – there are 110 within the City itself, plus 11 very close to it and 5 in Southwark. Because there are so many, there has been a lot of duplication of dedications, for example, there are at least twenty-two St Mary's churches (not counting St Mary Magdalen), eight St Martin's, eight St Michael's and five St Peter's. A number of saints are less popular and only have one church each, including St Helen, St Pancras, St Sithes and St Denis. The churches dedicated to popular saints usually have a suffix giving their location, such as St Andrew by the Wardrobe and St Olave Hart Street.

The following churches are exceptional:

St Helen's Bishopsgate

This was, at one time, probably Shakespeare's church because he appears in a 1597 tax assessment for the parish. It was originally the church of the priory of Benedictine nuns who wore a black habit with a cloak, cowl and veil. The church was divided into two parts, a church for the nuns on the north side, while the south half of the church was for the use of the parish. The two churches were divided by arches and screens, but the screens did not prevent the nuns from winking and waving to the parishoners – they were reproved for doing this in 1385. They were also in trouble for wearing ostentatious veils, kissing secular persons and for the number of children running about and the many small dogs kept by the prioress. In 1435, they were in trouble for dancing and revelling. Since the dissolution of the priory, the screens have been removed and it is one building. There are a number of things to view, including a squint to allow nuns who were sick or otherwise unable to attend church to view the elevation of the Host during Mass. There are also some fifteenth-century nuns' choir stalls with grotesque carved arm rests, as well as the night stairs which were used by the nuns to come down from their dormitory to sing Matins at about 3am. There are also important tombs, including that of Sir Thomas Gresham, who founded the Royal Exchange, Sir William Pickering, who was ambassador in Spain under Elizabeth, Sir Andrew Judd, Lord Mayor of London and founder of Tonbridge School, as well as the fifteenth-century tomb of Sir John and Lady Crosby. There is also the marvellous tomb of Captain Martin Bond who was commander of the City trained bands (militia) at Tilbury during the Armada crisis. He almost certainly heard Queen Elizabeth's famous speech rallying the troops, 'I am come amongst you, as you see, at this time, not for my recreation and disport, but being resolved, in the midst and heat of the battle, to live and die amongst you all; to lay down for my God, and for my kingdom, and my people, my honour and my blood, even in the dust.'

St Katherine Cree

Like St Helen's, the parishioners of St Katherine originally shared their church with a religious house – the Priory of the Holy Trinity, which was founded in 1108 by Matilda, the queen of Henry I, and was known as Christchurch. The church gets its curious name 'Cree', or 'Creechurch', from an old-fashioned pronunciation of Christ Church. The parishioners attended services at the altar of St Mary Magdalen in the south part of the priory church. The arrangement did not work well because the parish services were disturbed by the canons of the priory reciting their offices and so a separate church, the one that Shakespeare knew, was built in the priory churchyard sometime between 1280 and 1303. Even then there were still arguments between the parishioners and the canons from the priory and so in 1414 St Katherine's became a separate parish. The priory was dissolved in 1531 and the buildings given to Lord Audley who offered the priory church to the parishioners. According to Stow, 'having doubts in their heads about afterclaps', they turned down the offer. Nobody knows what Stow meant – afterclaps are the quieter random notes of bells after ringing. He might have meant that they were worried about taking on a former priory church in a time of political upheaval and unrest, or he might simply have meant that they were worried that the church was in a bad condition and would fall down on their heads. So they kept their original church, which is sadly very decayed. It is believed that Hans Holbein the Younger, the painter, may be buried here but the location of his grave is not known. He died during the plague outbreak of 1543 and may have been buried in a common grave. The great east window is said to be a copy of the one in Old St Paul's Cathedral.

St Bartholomew's Hospital and Churches

The two churches dedicated to St Bartholomew – the Great and the Less – and the hospital are located near to West Smithfield market. They were originally part of the Augustinian Priory of St Bartholomew, which was founded by Rahere in 1123. The only genuine information about Rahere comes from a book about the foundation of the priory written forty years after his death. This says that Rahere was a man 'born of low lineage' and with little learning who, as a youth, sought the patronage of the nobility, and inveigled his way into their households with japes and flattery until he became a familiar figure with both king and courtiers through

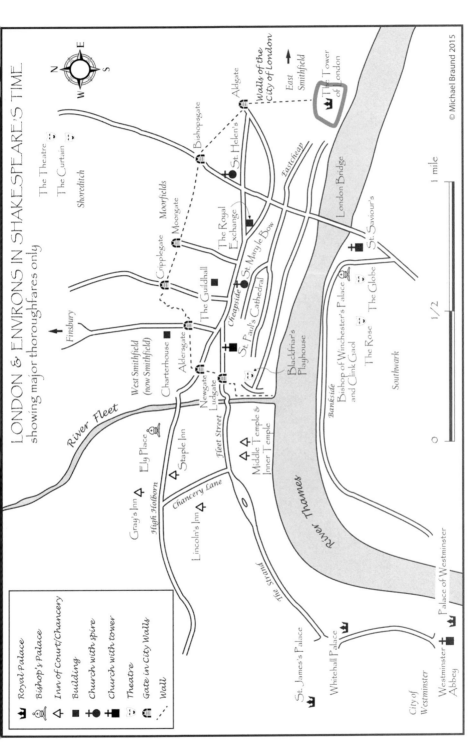

Map of Shakespeare's London and environs. *(Copyright Michael Braund, 2015)*

The pla= / iers names
By the Kings Ma:tis / plaiers :

Hallamas Day being the first of Nouembar A Play in the Banketinge house Called The Moor of Venis :

The poets / wch mayd the plaies

By his Ma:tis / plaiers :

The Sunday ffollowinge A play of the Merry wiues of winsor :.

By his Ma:tis / plaiers :.

On St stiuens night in the hall A play Called Mesur for Mesur :

Shaxberd

On St Jonns night A maske with musike presented by the Erl of Penbrok the Lord willowbie : 6 : knightes more of note : /

By his Ma:tis / plaiers :.

On Inosents night the plaie of Errors

Shaxberd :

By the Queens / Ma:tis plaiers :

On Sunday ffollowinge A plaie Called How to Larne of a woman to wooe

Hewood

The Boyes of = / the Chapell :.

On Newers Night A playe Cauled All ffoulles :

By Georg / Chapman

By his Ma:tis / plaiers :.

Betwin Newers Day And Twelfe day A play of Loues Labours Lost :

The Revels Account showing plays performed at court in the winter of 1604–5. (*The National Archives, AO3-908-13*)

Mr. WILLIAM
SHAKESPEARES

COMEDIES,
HISTORIES, &
TRAGEDIES.

Published according to the True Originall Copies.

Martin Droeshout sculpsit London.

LONDON

Printed by Isaac Iaggard, and Ed. Blount. 1623.

Shakespeare's portrait from the *First Folio* edition of Shakespeare's works.

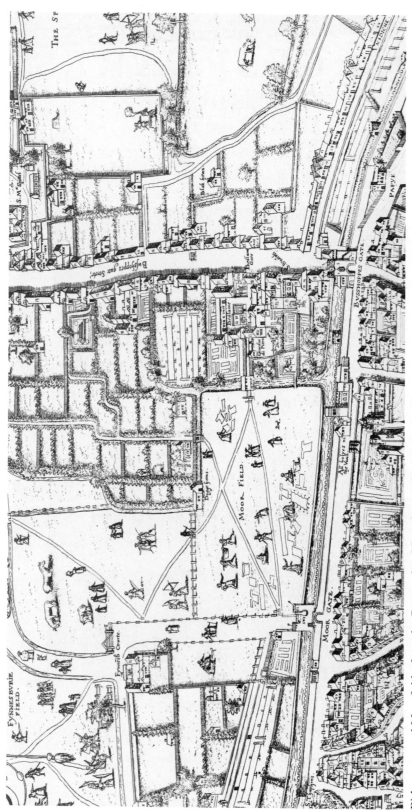

Bishopsgate and Moorfields, from the Copperplate Map, about 1559. (*Author's collection*)

Gateway to the Charterhouse, Charterhouse Square, London. (*Copyright Andrea Thomas, 2015*)

Replica of Bridewell Gateway, New Bridge Street, with head of Edward VI. (*Copyright Andrea Thomas, 2015*)

Plaque at location of original Globe theatre; the cartographer got the labels wrong – the Globe is the building labelled 'beere baiting'. *(Photograph Copyright Andrea Thomas, 2015)*

Plaque showing location of Aldermanbury Conduit, Love Lane. (*Copyright Andrea Thomas, 2015*)

London watchman with lantern, halberd and bell, frontispiece from Thomas Dekker, *The Bellman of London*, 1608.

Westminster showing the Eleanor Cross, Whitehall Palace, Westminster Hall and Westminster abbey, about 1560. (*Author's collection*)

his prominence in courtly revels. This Rahere was probably a canon of St Paul's Cathedral. People like a story and by the sixteenth century it was widely claimed that Rahere was King Henry I's court jester or minstrel.

The story goes on to say that the whole court was thrown into grief and gloom because of the loss in a winter storm of the *White Ship* which was carrying Henry's heir and a number of his friends. Following this tragedy, Rahere tired of court life and decided to go on a pilgrimage to Rome to seek forgiveness for his sins. While in Rome he fell dangerously ill and was nursed back to health by monks at the hospital of S. Giovanni di Dio on an island in the Tiber. He promised that if he recovered and returned home he would found a hospital for poor men. He did regain his health and on his way back he had a terrible dream in which he was seized by a beast with four feet and two wings which lifted him up and placed him on a ledge above a yawning pit. He cried out in fear and a figure who identified himself as St Bartholomew appeared at his side and said he had come to help, but in return Rahere was to found a church in his name in Smithfield.

When he returned to London, Rahere's friends advised him that Smithfield was part of the king's market. He approached the king who supported his project and work on the priory and hospital began in 1123 and Rahere became the first prior. The hospital had quite broad functions – in 1147 its charter defined it as being responsible for the needy, orphans, outcasts and the poor of the district, for every kind of sick person and for homeless wanderers. It was responsible for pregnant women until their child was born and for the care of children born in the hospital until they were 7 years old.

St Bartholomew the Great Church

A great priory church was built after Rahere's death, although it took nearly sixty years to complete as a result of shortages of money. The west front of the church faced onto Smithfield with, in front of it, a wall called the Cheyne, closed on market days by a chain to keep cattle out. The church was used by the canons of the priory, but the south transept was used by the local people as their parish church. The tomb of Rahere became a place of pilgrimage and many miracles were claimed to have occurred there. Succeeding priors continued to enhance the church. In the fourteenth century, a new Lady Chapel was built at the east end and Rahere's tomb was rebuilt and recoloured. In the early sixteenth century, Prior William Bolton built himself a splendid new lodging and a private chapel with a large window which overlooked the choir and high altar of the main church. Prior Bolton had his name on the window in the form of a rebus, a visual pun, with a barrel (tun) pieced by a crossbow bolt. In 1524, a rumour swept London that because of an astrological combination in the water signs great floods would sweep down and many would drown. There was a story that Prior Bolton fled the capital to Harrow on the Hill where he had laid in provisions for two months in case the floods came. John Stow claims the story is untrue.

Prior Bolton's regime was the end of the glory days for the priory. In 1539, it was abolished by Henry VIII and soon after was sold to Sir Richard Rich, head of the Court of Augmentations and the man responsible for carrying out the dissolution of the monasteries. He set out to plunder the church – the lead was removed from the roof, six bells were sold and the parish chapel, nave and north transept were pulled down. The west front was demolished except for the south-west doorway. A half-timbered house was built over it in 1559. After a brief period under Mary when the priory was restored, it was finally sold to Rich (by then Lord Rich) again and the Lady Chapel was converted to a house and the main priory buildings became large homes for the gentry.

What to See

The surviving parish church is the choir and south transept of the old church. You can see the curious mixture of styles which comes from centuries of tinkering, the famous window installed by Prior Bolton and the tombs of Rahere and Sir Walter Mildmay, who was Chancellor of the Exchequer under Queen Elizabeth. You can also see the surviving south-west doorway with a Tudor half-timbered house built over it.

There is a second church devoted to St Bartholomew, St Bartholomew the Less, which is situated within the hospital and acts as its parish church.

The Hospital

The dissolution of the priory had serious implications for London since the hospital provided essential services to the capital. After the Priory was dissolved, Henry VIII gave the hospital to the City of London together with an endowment; there was a collection at all the parish churches in the City and the hospital was restored. A similar process happened with St Thomas's hospital, which is south of the river. Dissolved by Henry VIII, it was acquired by the City of London in 1552 and given an endowment by Edward VI.

Whitehall Palace

This originally belonged to the Archbishops of York and was known as York Place. When Thomas Wolsey became archbishop, he extended it greatly so that it became the largest house in London. When Wolsey fell from power, Henry VIII acquired the property and extended it to become his official London residence. Henry was very keen on sports and he built tennis courts, bowling alleys and a cock pit there.

The palace is open to visitors who look sufficiently respectable. Paul Hentzner visited the palace in the reign of Queen Elizabeth and saw the royal library with books in Greek, Italian, French and Latin, including a small book written by Elizabeth when she was a child and dedicated to Henry VIII. He also saw the queen's writing cabinet, her bed, a jewel case covered in pearls, portraits and musical instruments, as well as a remarkable clock which consisted of a man riding a rhinoceros with four attendants who all bowed down when the clock struck the hour.

In the garden he saw a fountain with a sundial. While people were watching, a gardener turned a wheel and forced water out through many small nozzles sprinkling the spectators with water. Later, orange trees, aviaries and cages for wild animals were added and the place became known as Spring Garden.

The main hall and the banqueting hall were used for various entertainments, including masques and plays. Several of Shakespeare's plays were performed there. In 1597, *Love's Labour's Lost* was played there at Christmas before Queen Elizabeth – the first recorded performance. The Revels Accounts for 1604 record that the King's Majesty's players performed a play called *The Moor of Venice* in the banqueting house on 1 November – the first known performance of *Othello*. On 1 November 1611, *The Tempest*, the last play Shakespeare wrote on his own, was performed before King James and his courtiers at Whitehall.

St James's Palace

This fine Tudor palace was built by Henry VIII on the site of a hospital for fourteen women suffering from leprosy. The hospital had been dedicated to St James the Less and the palace took its name. It is smaller and less formal than the nearby Whitehall Palace and was a place where the monarchs could go to escape the pressures of court life. Anne Boleyn stayed there the night after her coronation and the initials HA (for Henry and Anne) entwined in a lovers' knot appear on a couple of Tudor fireplaces in the State apartments. Queen Mary was at St James's Palace in 1558 when she signed the treaty surrendering Calais. Elizabeth I was resident during the time of the Spanish Armada and set out from St James's to address her troops assembled at Tilbury, to the east of London.

Going Down the River: Greenwich and the *Golden Hind*

A trip down the river to Greenwich makes a good day out. On the way you will pass the *Golden Hind*, which is beached at Deptford. This is the ship in which Sir Francis Drake sailed round the world in 1577–80 and since then it has been on public display. According to Busino, it looks like the bleached ribs and bare skull of a dead horse.

Greenwich Palace itself was originally built by Humphrey, Duke of Gloucester, son of Henry IV, brother of Henry V and uncle of Henry VI. It was originally named the Palace of Placentia or the Palace of Pleasaunce. Henry VII rebuilt it and Henry VIII, Queen Mary and Queen Elizabeth were all born there and it became their main residence – Queen Elizabeth lived there in the summer enjoying the delightfulness of the situation.

There are a number of other attractions in addition to the palace itself. There is a deer park and a large aviary full of warblers which sing delightfully. There is also a very fine tower on the hill above the palace.

Visitors can sometimes get a pass to allow them to be admitted to the palace and to the presence chamber. Paul Hentzner visited during the last years of Elizabeth's reign and described the queen's procession to hear prayers. She was preceded by gentlemen, barons, earls and Knights of the Garter, all richly dressed and bareheaded. Then came the Chancellor carrying the seals of the kingdom in a red silk purse, while the royal sceptre and the sword of state were also carried in the procession. He described how the queen was able to talk to the ambassadors in English, French and Italian and also had a knowledge of Spanish and Dutch. People had to kneel when speaking to her and when she turned her face as she walked along, everybody she looked at had to kneel down. She was accompanied by the ladies of the court dressed in white and fifty gentlemen pensioners with gilt battle axes. She dined alone and her food was brought to her by a yeoman of the guard – a company of the tallest and stoutest men that can be found in England. The guard who brought her food had to taste it before Queen Elizabeth ate it. Some of the more formal aspects of life at court have changed under King James. People are no longer required to kneel when speaking to the monarch.

When Elizabeth was at Greenwich, the theatre companies would go down to perform before her. The Queen's Men, the Admiral's Men and the Lord Chamberlain's Men, which included Richard Burbage and William Shakespeare, all performed there. The theatre companies continued to perform there under King James and in 1613, a play called *Cardenio*, which was probably written by Shakespeare, was performed there for the ambassador of Savoy.

Going Up River: Richmond Palace, Hampton Court and Windsor Castle

There are three palaces along the river to the west of London: Richmond Palace, Hampton Court and Windsor.

Richmond Palace

There has been a royal palace at Richmond since 1399 when Edward I took his court there. At that time, it was known as Sheen Manor and the local town was Sheen. The palace was the favourite home of Richard II who took his bride, Anne of Bohemia, there. She died from plague there in 1394 and Richard was so distraught that he caused the house to be laid to waste. Henry V rebuilt the palace, but some of the buildings were destroyed by a fire in 1497 and Henry VII rebuilt it, naming it Richmond Palace after his title of Earl of Richmond in Yorkshire. Some people say that the hill there resembles one in Yorkshire. He died there.

Henry VIII also stayed at Richmond until he acquired the much more magnificent Hampton Court from the disgraced Cardinal Wolsey. Henry's first wife, Anne of Cleves, was given the palace as part of her divorce settlement. Queen Mary spent part of her honeymoon there and she kept her half-sister Elizabeth a prisoner there for a time. Queen Elizabeth enjoyed hunting deer in the great park there and the Office of Works built a stage and tiered seating to allow plays to be performed. All the major acting companies played there in the 1580s and 1590s and it is possible that Shakespeare performed there. Queen Elizabeth died at Richmond in 1603. King James is not fond of Richmond, but his elder son, Prince Henry, commissioned large water features for the gardens before his death in 1612.

Hampton Court

Hampton Court is a few miles further up river from Richmond. It was originally a manor belonging to the order of St John of Jerusalem and was acquired by Cardinal Wolsey. He spent a huge fortune on building a magnificent Tudor palace. After Wolsey lost Henry VIII's confidence the king took over the building and expanded it further, adding the huge kitchens, the great hall and a royal tennis court. The palace was used for the performance of plays including Shakespeare's *A Midsummer Night's Dream*, which was acted there on 1 January 1603.

Hampton Court is certainly worth visiting. Paul Hentzner went there late in Elizabeth's reign and saw the presence chamber, the queen's private chapel and her bedchamber. He remarked on her bed covered with costly coverlets of silk.

Thomas Platter visited Hampton Court in 1599 he said that it is 'the finest and most magnificent royal edifice to be found in England or for that matter in other countries'. He was particularly impressed by the gardens and remarked on a beautiful sundial and lunar clock and described a fine large fountain 'with an excellent water work with which one may spray any ladies or others standing around and wet them well'. He also admired the topiary in the gardens:

> there were all manner of shapes, men and women, half men and half horse, lillies and delicate crenellations all round made from dry twigs bound together and the afore-said evergreen quick set shrubs, or entirely of rosemary, all true to the life, and so cleverly and amusingly interwoven, mingled and grown together, trimmed and arranged picture-wise so that their equal would be hard to find.

There were poles in the gardens supporting wooden heraldic beasts. By the river is the Mount Garden which was crowned by the Great Round Arbour – a glass building topped with a lead cupola, surmounted with the king's beasts and a great gilded crown. The arbour gave views across the river and also looked down on the gardens.

Inside the palace, he saw the queen's quarters, the banqueting hall and the Paradise Chamber with a ceiling adorned with beautiful paintings and a canopy with precious stones where the monarch sits in state. In the library, he saw a unicorn's horn. Platter was keen on music and he described the palace's collection of musical instruments, organs and positive (smaller moveable) organs and virginals, including one with gold and silver strings which was played by the queen. He was allowed to play the organ in the chapel.

Visiting Hampton Court is expensive. Platter had three guides, one who showed him round at the start of his visit, to whom he gave a gratuity, then a gardener who showed him the gardens, who also got a tip. Finally, he was shown the rest of the palace by the wife and daughter of the governor of the palace. At the end of his visit, he was invited for a morning drink with the governor and having made a gift to his ladies left Hampton Court.

Windsor Castle

The castle dates back to William the Conqueror and, although it retained its military capacity, it was changed into a luxurious palace by Edward III. Visitors are told that two of the courts that form part of the castle were paid for from the ransoms that were paid by King David II of Scotland and King John II (John the Good) of France. The Tudors continued to stay at the castle and Elizabeth undertook an extensive programme of refurbishment.

Edward VI disliked Windsor, its absence of gardens making him feel that he was in a prison. Elizabeth enjoyed spending time there and used it for diplomatic meetings and for hunting – one of her favourite pursuits. King James uses the castle primarily as a base for hunting. Windsor is a relatively small castle as compared with the more modern ones and there are frequent quarrels between courtiers over who should have which room.

For the visitor, the most important sight is St George's Chapel, the vast cathedral-like church that is the Chapel of the Order of the Garter and where Henry VI, Edward IV and Henry VIII were buried. It became a major destination for pilgrims in the Middle Ages since it housed a fragment of Christ's Cross and the body of John Schorne, a holy man and Vicar of North Marston in Buckinghamshire who was known for miraculous cures for gout and toothache, for discovering a miraculous well and for casting the Devil into a boot.

The castle is most famous as the headquarters of the Order of the Garter; this is an order of chivalry founded by Edward III sometime between 1344 and 1348. Membership was limited to the king and twenty-five knights. The members wear a velvet mantle, a Tudor bonnet with a feather, a gold collar, a figure of St George on horseback slaying a dragon and a garter that is worn below the left knee – inscribed with the words *Honi soit qui mal y pense*.

The origins of the name of the order are not known. Originally, Edward had planned to set up an Order of the Knights of the Round Table based on King Arthur and built a circular building at Windsor to house it, but changed his mind. Various legends account for the origin of the order. The most popular account involves the Countess of Salisbury, who while dancing at a ball discovered her garter had slipped from her leg. While the courtiers were sniggering, the king picked it up and returned it to her and said, *Honi soit qui mal y pense* ('Shame on him who thinks evil of it'), this phrase became the motto of the order.

Every year, a feast is held to induct new members into the order and Shakespeare's *The Merry Wives of Windsor* may have been written for the feast in 1597. It is sometimes claimed that Queen Elizabeth had enjoyed the character of Falstaff in *Henry IV* so much that she commanded Shakespeare to write another play showing Falstaff in love and *The Merry Wives of Windsor* was his response. In Act Five, Mistress Quickly gives a speech in which she tells the fairies to spruce up the castle to prepare for the Garter ceremony:

> About, about;
> Search Windsor Castle, elves, within and out:
> Strew good luck, ouphes, on every sacred room:
> That it may stand till the perpetual doom,
> In state as wholesome as in state 'tis fit,
> Worthy the owner, and the owner it.
> The several chairs of order look you scour
> With juice of balm and every precious flower:
> Each fair instalment, coat, and several crest,
> With loyal blazon, evermore be blest!
> And nightly, meadow-fairies, look you sing,

Like to the Garter's compass, in a ring:
The expressure that it bears, green let it be,
More fertile-fresh than all the field to see;
And 'Honi soit qui mal y pense' write
In emerald tufts, flowers purple, blue and white;

There is a more junior order, called the Poor Knights of Windsor, which consists of old and poor men who are given a pension and meals and whose duties are to attend the chapel twice a day and pray for the safety of the sovereign and the happy administration of the country.

As well as the chapel, visitors to Windsor are shown Queen Elizabeth's bedchamber and the beds of Henry VII, Henry VIII, Edward VI and Anne Boleyn.

Chapter Five

Entertainment

Lﬁondon is a great place for popular entertainment, whether it is
public ceremonies, pleasure gardens, watching or participating
in sport, music and dancing, street entertainment or even bear
baiting, there is something to appeal to everybody.

One popular pursuit with Londoners is simply to stroll in Moor Fields
to the north of the City. According to Grenade, 'on feast days it is full of
people of every age and gender. Some practice archery there ... Others,
among the rest of the people there, stroll so as to enjoy the beauty and
good air of the place.' Perhaps you could follow your stroll with a visit to a
tavern where you might meet many of your fellow countrymen.

There are a number of ceremonies or public entertainments that are
well worth going to see.

Accession Day Tilts

Queen Elizabeth came to the throne on 17 November and from the 1580s,
a great jousting tournament was held in the tiltyard in Whitehall Palace
to celebrate her anniversary. Thousands of people attend these spectacles
and the public are admitted for a fee of 12*d*. Since King James came to
the throne, these spectacles have been held on the anniversary of his
accession, 24 March.

Knights participating in the tournament arrive in pageant cars or on
horseback, disguised as some hero from classical times or the Arthurian
stories or even as rustic figures – Sir Philip Sidney appeared at the 1581
tilt as a Shepherd Knight and on one occasion there was a Frozen Knight.
The knights' servants are dressed in costumes that are in harmony with
the characters adopted by their masters – Sidney's servants dressed as

shepherds, for example. Once the knights have arrived, a squire presents a shield decorated with the character's device to the monarch and explains the significance of his disguise in prose or poetry. Entrants go to a great deal of trouble and expense to devise themes and acquire suitable costumes for their followers. Some even hire poets or dramatists to write the explanations of their theme and hire actors to speak their words. A few use the occasion as a means of apologising to the monarch for any errors they may have committed.

Lord Mayor's Day

On 29 September every year, one of the alderman is elected by the liverymen of London as Lord Mayor and the day he takes office (usually 28 October) is one of parades and celebrations. It starts with the new Lord Mayor going by water to take the oath of allegiance before the Lord Chancellor. His boat is accompanied by a flotilla of highly decorated ships, galleys, brigantines and foists, while each of the livery companies has its own highly decorated barge.

The Lord Mayor returns to the City by boat and then the fun really starts. The artillery men from the Tower set up a train of gunpowder in St Paul's churchyard with a small iron gun every 6ft. This is ignited when the Lord Mayor approaches and, according to Grenade, 'they sing such a song that it seems as if the great church of St Paul's might fall to the ground and there is not a house even in the uttermost surroundings which does not shake vigorously'. A small boat equipped with sixteen pieces of ordnance is moored in the Thames and fires a salute six times during the day.

There is then a huge parade along Cheapside to the Guildhall. This lasts from 8am until 1pm and includes the princes and lords of the council and the liverymen from the Lord Mayor's company. The liverymen from the other companies line the streets. They are all dressed in hoods and livery over long robes of black cloth lined with fine sables and edged with velvet. The more junior members of the companies – the bachelors – are also present in fur trimmed gowns, while there are a number of poor men dressed in blue gowns with red sleeves and caps carrying small shields with the arms of the companies. Each company appoints a number of whifflers – gentlemen ushers who wear velvet gowns, golden chains and carry white staffs to ensure that the bachelors and poor men behave properly.

The Archbishop of Canterbury rides in the parade on horseback accompanied by the mace bearers, earls, marquises, lords and senior courtiers. The new mayor and his predecessor, dressed in scarlet robes trimmed with fur, ride on fine horses with velvet harnesses covered with gilded buttons and wearing gilded horseshoes. They are preceded by the sword bearer dressed in gold chains and rings and jewels, carrying a sword in a white velvet scabbard studded with fine and rich pearls. They are followed by the aldermen in similar gowns.

The crowd is kept under control by the city marshal on horseback, accompanied by two footmen in livery and a group of youths and men armed with fencing swords. There are also men wearing masks like giants who try to keep the procession route clear.

Apart from the dignitaries, there is a great deal else to amuse the crowd. There are floats called pageants with different themes. In 1617, the theme was India and lads threw dates, nutmegs, ginger and sugar confections into the crowds of spectators. There were lots of musicians and people dressed as animals. People in the buildings in Cheapside threw squibs and crackers into the crowd.

The parade ends at Guildhall where there is a magnificent feast and at 3pm there is a further procession to St Paul's to hear divine service. After the service, it is beginning to get dark, the streets are quieter and there is a torch-light parade accompanied by music.

The parades attract every sort of person, and according to Horatio Busino, the crowds include old men 'in their dotage; insolent youths and boys, especially the apprentices; painted wenches and women of the lower classes carrying their children all anxious to see the show'. The spectacle is a fantastic piece of free entertainment.

Very few people dare to go by coach to the procession because, according to Busino, 'the insolence of the mob is extreme. They cling behind the coaches and should the coachman use his whip, they jump down and pelt him with mud.'

The whole event is immensely enjoyable, as reported by Grenade, 'To conclude, there is nothing in this day which, in a manner of speaking, should not be merry. Which is to say that after this excellent spectacle, the people retire as joyous and happy as they could possibly be.'

Festivals

May Day

This used to be a great celebration in London and featured a huge maypole which was set up near St Andrew Undershaft. Many other parishes had maypoles. Sadly, two things happened. First, there was a riot against foreigners on May Day 1517, the so-called Evil May Day and this made the celebration unpopular with the authorities. Second, the Puritans disliked the pagan aspects of the festival and in 1547, Sir Stephen, the curate of St Katherine Cree, which is just down the road from St Andrew Undershaft, preached that the maypole was an idol. The people outside whose houses the pole was kept cut it into pieces and burned it. Nevertheless, the tradition of young people going out into the fields to fetch May blossoms very early on May Day morning continues. Shakespeare refers to this in *Henry VIII*:

'tis as much impossible
To scatter 'em as 'tis to make 'em sleep
On May-day morning, which will never be.
We may as well push against Paul's [i.e., push over St Paul's Cathedral] as
    stir 'em.

Frost Fair

The climate seems to be getting much colder and this has led to the Thames freezing on a couple of occasions. In 1564, the river froze on 21 December and many Londoners went on the ice, including Queen Elizabeth who went there daily and shot at targets. The ice melted on 3 January and by 5 January there was none to be seen.

In 1607, there was a sharp frost in late December, so that people could walk on the ice until 3 January 1608. There was then a severe frost between 10 and 15 January. A real frost fair was set up. People danced and went bowling on the ice, stalls were erected for the sale of fruit, beer and wine. Fires were lit in hearths to toast bread and heat sack. A barber set up in business and many people queued up to be shaved because, as it was said, to have been shaved on the Thames was something to be remembered in after life.

Sports

Londoners are very keen on a whole range of sports. Fencing is popular and is an essential skill for the more wealthy gentlemen in case they are challenged to a duel. There are a number of fencing schools in London in Ely Place, the Artillery Gardens, Leadenhall and Smithfield. Fencing performances are put on at large pubs such as the Belle Sauvage in Ludgate Hill or the Bull in Bishopsgate and also at the Curtain Theatre in Shoreditch. A book by the Italian Giacomo di Grassi, *The true arte of defence*, was published in English in 1594. It is a kind of self-help manual regarding the use of swords, rapiers, daggers, two-handed swords, staffs and pikes, as well as other weapons. Sword fighting is a dangerous pastime and in 1562 a fencer was accidentally killed in a display in the Bell tavern. In 1604, Robert Crichton, Lord Sanquhar, was injured in the eye by a fencing master, John Turner, and in 1612 he hired two men to kill Turner, one of them, called Robert Carlisle, shot and killed him. Carlisle and his accomplice were soon caught and hanged. Sanquhar fled but King James offered a reward for him alive or dead. He was eventually arrested, tried and hanged outside Westminster Hall.

Football is not quite as violent but is equally popular with Londoners. It is played in the streets with a pig's bladder filled with peas. Shakespeare is certainly familiar with the game because he mentions it in *The Comedy of Errors*, describing a leather ball.

> Am I so round with you as you with me,
> That like a football you do spurn me thus?
> You spurn me hence, and he will spurn me hither:
> If I last in this service, you must case me in leather.

Some writers disapprove of football, Philip Stubbes, the Puritan writer, commenting:

> I protest vnto you, it may rather bee called a friendly kind of fight, than a play or recreation. A bloody and murthering practice than a fellowly sport or pastime. For doth not every one lie in wait for his aduersary seeking to overthrow him and to picke him on his nose ... [so that] sometimes their legs are broken, sometimes their armes, sometimes one part thrust out of joint, sometime another, sometimes their noses gush with blood.

A game involving throwing a ball at a target is also popular. Horatio Busino described how 'the lads throw the ball in the street, aiming at a mark according to certain rules, females also taking part with them, as they also like to have a little capering on feast days'.

The wealthier portion of society takes part in hunting. Henry VIII, Queen Elizabeth and King James have all been enthusiastic hunters, enjoying pursuing deer in their royal parks and when on progresses round the country. King James is particularly keen and there have been complaints by courtiers and ambassadors that the business of government grinds to a halt while the king is away chasing deer. Henry and Elizabeth had to cut down on their hunting on horseback as they grew older, but were able to enjoy another version of the sport called drive hunting where they would stand in a specially constructed building and shoot with crossbows at deer that were driven past them. Most nobles and many gentry have enclosed parks which are used to keep herds of deer. In about 1600 there were about 850 parks in England and Wales ranging in size from 20 to 1,000 acres. In London, it is possible, if you have the right contacts to go hunting with hounds in the Forest of Middlesex around Highgate and Hampstead.

Other types of hunting are popular, including hawking with falcons or goshawks, hunting hares with hounds and even hunting ducks with dogs. Ducks are put in water and pursued by dogs – the ducks who are in their natural element usually escape. Henry VIII was keen on angling, while King James has two cormorants that are used to catch fish – the birds have laces round their necks to prevent them from swallowing the fish. Hunting is mainly for the rich. For the poor in rural areas, there is always the possibility of some poaching – there are even rumours (probably unfounded) that William Shakespeare had to leave Stratford because he had been caught poaching.

Wrestling is popular as a spectator sport, particularly during Bartholomew Fair. Archery is, in theory, compulsory for able-bodied men, but guns have been taking over from the longbow for many years and the practice of archery is in decline. John Stow said, 'What should I speake of this ancient dayly exercises in the longbow by citizens of this citie, now almost cleane left off and forsaken.'

Gambling

There are many opportunities for gambling in London which range across a whole gamut of activities. Some aristocrats are very keen on arranging races between picked servants. These are run over long distances – 15 or 20 miles and large sums are bet on the result. King James is very keen on these events and took the winner of one race into his service.

Most aristocrats have bowling greens in their gardens and they are found in royal palaces, while indoor alleys are found in London. Bowling is closely associated with gambling and there are professional cheats who will lure innocent travellers into betting on fixed games of bowls. John Stow complained that 'now of late so many bowling alleys and other houses for unlawful gaming hath been raised in other parts of the city and its suburbs'. He described More Lane in the parish of St Giles in Moorfield which used to be inhabited by bowyers, fletchers and bow-string makers but it was 'now little occupied, archery giving way to a number of bowling-alleys and dicing houses which in all places are increased and too much frequented'. Aaron Holland, builder of the Red Bull Playhouse in Clerkenwell, owned a common bowling alley that also housed dicing, tabling and carding.

Royal tennis is also very popular. The game involves serving the balls on to a penthouse – a small shelf that runs along one side of the court – and the ball is then returned across the net. Henry VII was an amazingly good player and had courts built in his palaces at Richmond, Woodstock, Windsor and Westminster, while Cardinal Wolsey built a court at Hampton Court. There is also a court on the site of the house of the Crutched Friars in Aldgate. The tennis courts have windows with wire netting so spectators can watch the matches. Like bowling, there is often betting on the outcome of tennis matches and Gilbert Walker, in his *Manifest Discoverie of the most vyle and detestable use of dyce play*, claims that one man lost £600 on tennis in a week. There is a story that Anne Boleyn was gambling on a tennis match when she was arrested and taken to the Tower.

Indoor games are popular at night and there are a whole raft of these including dice, cards, chess, tables (backgammon), dames (draughts), billiards and fox and geese. Even Queen Elizabeth enjoyed playing cards for money. It is probably wise to lose when playing against her. In 1596, Lord North recorded in his accounts that he had lost £32 playing cards with the queen. This seems to have helped his career, since he was appointed as Treasurer of the Royal Household in the same year.

Merrells or Nine Men's Morris is popular and was played by monks – boards are found carved into cloister seats in a number of cathedrals, although whether the worldly monks gambled on the outcome of their games is not recorded. Giant outdoor boards were sometimes cut into village greens. In *A Midsummer Night's Dream*, Titania mentions this practice when describing the impact of a flood:

> The ox hath therefore stretch'd his yoke in vain,
> The ploughman lost his sweat, and the green corn
> Hath rotted ere his youth attain'd a beard;
> The fold stands empty in the drowned field,
> And crows are fatted with the murrion flock;
> The nine men's morris is fill'd up with mud,

Music and Dancing

Music is very popular in England and is played in many places around London. Queen Elizabeth had a great love for music; she was skilled at playing the virginals, supported a number of composers and employed twenty-nine musicians. Dinner at court was announced by twelve trumpets and two drums.

Gentlemen are all expected to be able to sight read and to play the viol or the lute. Some gentlemen have a great interest in music. When Sir Thomas Kitson of Hengrave Hall in Suffolk died a few years ago in 1602, his possessions included fifty-four song books, some books of dance music, twelve viols, seven recorders, four lutes, five virginals, brass and woodwind instruments and two great organs. He employed a number of musicians, led by John Wilbye who published two books of madrigals. Madrigals, which are unaccompanied part songs for three to eight voices, are hugely popular and have been since the 1580s when Nicholas Yonge published a collection of English translations of some Italian ones. Now the most fashionable English composers, John Bull, William Byrde, Thomas Campion, John Dowland and Orlando Gibbons, write them.

If you attend a play you will probably hear an hour-long concert before it begins. In 1602, the Duke of Stettin-Pomerania attended a play and heard a concert with organs, lutes, pandores (a kind of large bass mandolin), mandolins, violins and flute. All of Shakespeare's plays except *The Comedy of Errors* contain music and some of his songs such as 'Full Fathom Five' and 'Where the Bee Sucks' from *The Tempest* (set to music by Robert Johnson) and 'It was a Lover and his Lass' (set to music by Thomas Morley) from *Twelfth Night* are justly famous. In 1598, the theatre company the Admiral's Men employed at least eight musicians and owned three trumpets, one drum, one treble viol, one bass viol, one pandore, one sackbut, three tymbrels and some bells. There are some fairly standard musical effects, the arrival of a king is accompanied by hoyboes (oboes), a drum heard offstage would represent a marching army, while a trumpet and drum could sound the alarm or a retreat.

Church music is still popular in London. The singers of the Chapel Royal perform elaborate music written by William Byrd and Thomas Tallis, while psalm singing is also very well liked; huge crowds go to Paul's Cross in St Paul's churchyard to sing psalms. According to Hentzner, the English are very fond of loud noises such as cannon, drums and ringing bells, 'so that it is common for a number of them that have got a glass in their heads, to go up into some belfry and ring the bells for hours together for the sake of exercise'. Sometimes there are competitions between different churches to see which bells make the most noise or can be heard the furthest away.

There is a lot of popular music – printed ballads are often sold in the streets and these cover a wide range of subject from news to ribaldry; about 3,000 were published in the second half of the sixteenth century. Most are written to be sung to popular tunes of the day, such as 'Greensleeves'. There are also street musicians, minstrels who perform at feasts, weddings and wakes and others who play tunes in taverns and alehouses for a few coppers. You are never far from the sound of music in the City of London. Stephen Gosson, a poet and dramatist, complained in 1579 that 'London is so full of unprofitable pipers and fiddlers that a man can no sooner enter a tavern than two or three cast of them hang at his heels to give him a dance before he departs'. Unfortunately, minstrels are sometimes in league with pickpockets – the musician will distract the audience while the pickpocket gets to work.

The street musicians are closely related to other street entertainers, fencers, tightrope walkers and jugglers. Reginald Scot, in his *Discoverie of Witchcraft*, described the tricks performed by what he calls jugglers:

> The true art therefore of juggling consisteth in legierdemaine; to wit, the nimble conveiance of the hand, which is especiallie performed three waies. The first and principall consisteth in hiding and conveieng of balles, the second in the alteration of monie, the third in the shuffeling of the cards. He that is expert in these may shew much pleasure, and manie feats, and hath more cunning than all other witches or magicians.

Sometimes there were more elaborate tricks. Scot described one in which a juggler was stabbed with a dagger and bled profusely but then recovered. The trick was that the juggler wore a metal plate under his clothing and a bladder full of sheep or calf's blood. The bladder would burst spectacularly but the plate would prevent the dagger from piercing his skin. Scot described one incident where a juggler demonstrated the trick 'at a tavern in Cheapside from whence he presentlie went into Powle's churchyard and died. Which misfortune fell upon him through his own follie, as being then drunken, and having forgotten his plate which he should have had for his defence.'

Bear Baiting and Cock Fighting

Londoners have an unpleasant love of watching animals fighting. Henry VIII was keen on cock fighting and built an elaborate cock pit at Whitehall which was octagonal with decorations of stone beasts holding iron standards and a weather vane in the shape of a lion. It had three tiers of seating. There are a number of cock pits in the City of London in Jewin Lane, St Giles in the Fields and Shoe Lane. Thomas Platter visited the one in Shoe Lane:

> There is also in the city of London not far from the horse-market, which occupies a large site, a house where cock-fights are held annually throughout three quarters of the year (for in the remaining quarter they told me it was impossible since the feathers are full of blood), and I saw the place, which is built like a theatre. In the centre on the floor stands a circular table covered with straw and with ledges round it, where the cocks are teased and incited to fly at one another, while those with wagers as to which cock will win sit closest around the circular disk, but the spectators who are merely present on their entrance penny sit around higher up, watching with eager pleasure the fierce and angry fight between the cocks, as these wound each other to death with spurs and beaks. And the party whose cock surrenders or dies loses the wager; I am told that stakes on a cock often amount to many thousands of crowns, especially if they have reared the cock themselves and brought their own along. For the

master who inhabits the house has many cocks besides, which he feeds in separate cages and keeps for this sport, as he showed us. He also had several cocks, none of which he would sell for less than twenty crowns; they are very large but just the same kind as we have in our country. He also told us that if one discovered that the cocks' beaks had been coated with garlic, one was fully entitled to kill them at once. He added too, that it was nothing to give them brandy before they began to fight, adding what wonderful pleasure there was in watching them.

Fights are bloody affairs where cocks are divided into teams and fight individually until there is only one left. Worse is the battle royal when a large number of cocks are put in the pit together and left to fight until only one survives. Gervase Markham, the soldier, poet and writer, published a work in 1614 called the *Choice, Ordering and Breeding and Dyeting of the Fighting Cocke* in which he said 'there is no pleasure more noble, delightsome or voyd of cozenage and deceipt than this pleasure of cocking'. Many fighting cocks are bred in Norfolk and in 1607 George Wilson, Vicar of Wretham in that county, championed the pastime in a work entitled *The Commendation of Cocke and Cock-fighting wherein is shewed that cockefighting was before the coming of Christ*.

King James is an enthusiastic patron of the 'sport'. He appointed a 'cockmaster', a royal officer who was responsible for the breeding, feeding and training of gamecocks for fighting in the royal cock pit. Throughout his reign cockfighting has been a favourite pastime of the king. In the spring of 1617, when he paid a visit in state to the city of Lincoln, he directed that a 'cocking' should take place at an inn yard in his presence, and 'appointed four cocks to be put in the pit together, which made his Majesty very merry'.

Bear and bull baiting is also hugely popular in England. Queen Elizabeth enjoyed the sport, as does King James. In some places it is more popular than going to church. According to Sir Thomas More, at Beverley, many of the people were at a bear baiting at the time of evensong when the church fell down and crushed some people who were inside. 'A good fellow that after heard the tale told, "So" quod he, "now may you see what it is to be at evensong when you should be at the bear baiting".'

The bear or bull is tied to a post with a short rope and then bulldogs are encouraged to attack it, sometimes the dogs are crushed by the bear or tossed by the bull. The bear can 'pinch' or claw the dogs, sometimes killing them. Grenade saw a bear fight fourteen mastiffs, of which it killed two. Sometimes the displays end with the dogs pursuing a horse running free with an ape on its back. Robert Laneham wrote a letter in 1575 describing a bear baiting that took place when the queen visited Kenilworth:

Thursday, the fourteenth of July, and the sixth day of her Majesty's coming, a great sort of bandogs [mastiffs] were then tied in the outer court and thirteen bears in the inner ... It was a sport very pleasant, of these beasts, to see the bear with his pink eyes leering after his enemies approach, the nimbleness and wayt [watchfulness] of the dog to take his advantage, and the force and experience of the bear again to avoid the assaults. If he were bitten in one place, how he would pinch in another to get free, that if he were taken once, then what shift, with biting, with clawing, with roaring, tossing and tumbling, he would work to wind himself free from them. And when he was loose, to shake his ears twice or thrice with the blood and the slather about his physiognomy, was a matter of goodly relief.

Bear, bulls and apes are expensive and the matches are arranged to ensure that they survive the contests. In about 1564, Richard Wood bought a bear cub from John Seckerston of Nantwich, for the sum of £3 13s. 4d. Seckerston seems to have been a member of a bear-owning family, the Earl of Derby's bearward was called John Sakarston. Currently, the most famous bear of all is called 'Sackerson' and he is mentioned in *The Merry Wives of Windsor* when Slender, who is trying to impress Anne Page, says, 'I have seen Sackerson loose twenty times, and have taken him by the chain; but, I warrant you, the women have so cried and shrieked at it, that it passed: but women, indeed, cannot abide 'em; they are very ill-favoured rough things.' Sackerson's Tudor predecessor as most famous bear was called 'Harry Hunks'.

The arena for bear baiting in London is located in Paris Garden in Southwark. It includes kennels for mastiffs, three of which can hold down a bear and four a lion. In 1590, its stock included three bulls, nine bears (five great bears, one bear, one she bear and an old bear), a horse and an ape. By 1611 it had acquired two white bears and a lion. Admission is very cheap: 1*d*. to get in and 2*d*. to go into the stands. It is, however, potentially very dangerous. In 1594, a bear broke loose in the bear garden and attacked a man who subsequently died. Bulls can toss angry mastiffs high up into the galleries.

Bear baiting is a royal monopoly and the Privy Council supports it as a way of keeping the people entertained. When, in the summer of 1583, the Privy Council ordered the Corporation of London to enforce the laws for the practice of archery, the Lord Mayor, in reply, laid the blame for the neglect of shooting with bows on the growing vogue of bear baiting. But the court and upper classes took another view of the situation. The sport was defended as 'a sweet and comfortable recreation fitted for the solace and comfort of a peaceable people'. In 1591, the growth of theatres on the Bankside was creating a formidable competition with the attractions of Paris Garden. The Privy Council forbade the opening of theatres on Thursdays, so as to promote public support on that day of 'the game of bearbaiting and like pastimes which are maintained by her Majesty's pleasure' and were suffering neglect.

In 1604, Edward Alleyn, the actor and theatre proprietor, and his father-in-law, Philip Henslowe, bought the royal office of Master of the Game of Bears, Bulls and Dogs. Clearly, they regard these animal sports as very important because they seem to devote as much of their time to them as they do to the theatre. In 1613, the Hope Theatre was built on Bankside by Philip Henslowe and is used as a dual purpose bear-baiting establishment and play house.

Shakespeare is clearly familiar with bear baiting and there are many references to it in his plays. For example, Richard III compared his father, the Duke of York, in battle to a baited bear (*Henry VI, Part III*):

Methought he bore him in the thickest troop
As doth a lion in a herd of neat
Or as a bear encompass'd round with dogs
Who having pinch'd a few and made them cry
The rest stand all aloof, and bark at him

London has very many opportunities for entertainment and visitors and residents alike take full advantage of them. Some spend rather too much time on leisure pursuits. In *Twelfth Night*, Sir Andrew Aguecheek regretted his lack of knowledge of languages, 'I would I had bestowed that time in the tongues that I have in fencing, dancing, and bear-baiting.'

Theatres

Since the 1530s London has seen an amazing growth in the number of theatres and the range of plays that are on offer. In the early days, actors began hiring halls in which to perform. Then they began performing in the courtyards of inns and some inns were converted into theatres. In 1586, the first purpose-built theatre was constructed in Shoreditch and since then we have seen the development of new theatres in the north of the City, Blackfriars and, most notably, across the river in Southwark. The new theatres offer an enormous range of plays, old and new and there are some fantastic playwrights working in the metropolis. This huge flowering could not have happened without the development of an audience and theatre-going is now a regular activity for both Londoners and the many visitors to the capital. It has been estimated that in the 1590s, 15,000 people a week went to the theatre – a large number when you remember that London's population was only about 200,000. As well as performing in theatres, the acting companies put on plays at court and in the halls of the Inns of Court, particularly in the days after Christmas. They also go on tour round the country.

The theatres operate in a curious situation. The City government, which is sometimes influenced by Puritan thinking, does not like them much – partly because they are associated with prostitution and vice but more because they are seen as threats to public order and, equally importantly, because they create noise, disturbance and traffic congestion in their neighbourhoods. There have been constant complaints about the traffic chaos caused by coaches taking people to the Blackfriars Theatre. Central government in the form of the Privy Council has a contradictory attitude. On the one hand, they see theatres as potentially dangerous sources of radical ideas and as potent focuses of popular unrest, and on occasion they have banned plays that they see as seditious and they stopped plays being performed in pubs in 1600. On the other hand, some members of the council, such as the Earl of Leicester, had their own companies of players and all Privy Councillors are very well aware that Queen Elizabeth was an ardent fan of the theatre and King James is even more so. Both monarchs enjoyed seeing plays put on at court at Christmas and Easter. Royal patronage means that the Privy Council cannot interfere too much with the theatres' business. So they continue to prosper in a sort of no-man's-land. Not quite approved of by officialdom, but having powerful voices at court. Perhaps that is how it should be.

The big problem that faces theatre companies is the plague. As soon as the disease makes its appearance, the theatres are shut to prevent too many people gathering together and spreading the infection. This happened in 1592–4, 1603 and 1608. Curiously, although the worst aspects of human life are depicted on the stage – murder, incest, civil war, betrayal and the deliberate blinding of people, the symptoms of the plague and its victims are never portrayed in the London theatres – a step too far even for the dramatists.

The Companies
In the sixteenth century, the government was very concerned about the problem of sturdy beggars – people who were healthy enough to support themselves, but who chose not to work in a regular job and either begged or stole or made money in unconventional ways as street entertainers or actors. A particular concern was masterless men who had left their parish of birth and wandered off to seek work. In 1572, a harsh Act of Parliament was introduced which tried to deal with a number of aspects

of this problem. It ordered that all fencers, bearwards, common players of interludes and minstrels (not belonging to any baron of this realm, or to any other honourable person of greater degree) wandering abroad without the licence of two justices were to be 'grievously whipped and burned through the gristle of the right ear with a hot iron of the compass of an inch about'. That was for a first offence. A second offence resulted in the person being convicted as a felon and the third the death penalty.

The Act was somewhat softened in 1597 when the penalty was reduced to whipping and sending the masterless man back to his parish of origin. The effect of this legislation was that, in future, actors had to be members of permanent companies of players under the patronage of great nobles. At the same time, members of the nobility enjoyed the status of having their own companies of actors. It gave them an opportunity to enhance their prestige and status and, since the queen was fond of watching plays, a chance to impress her and win her favour. As a result, theatre companies were set up under the patronage of many nobles: the Earls of Leicester, Sussex, Warwick, Essex and Oxford.

King James is even keener on the theatre than Queen Elizabeth and when he came to the throne, it was decided that acting companies would, in future, need to be under royal patronage and he has taken the Lord Chamberlain's Men under his wing, while his wife, Queen Anne, his sons, Prince Henry and Prince Charles, and his daughter, Princess Elizabeth, also have their own companies.

Although the companies are under royal patronage, much of the London theatre is controled by impresarios, men who build theatres and finance theatre companies, as well as act in plays. The leading impresarios are Philip Henslowe and his son-in-law, the actor and businessman Edward Alleyn, and their rivals, the Burbage brothers, Richard, who is also an actor, and Cuthbert. The Burbages' father, James, was also an impresario and the first man to establish a purpose-built theatre in London.

What is extraordinary about the leading companies is the amount of work they undertake. The London theatre is not about long runs of successful plays, instead, the major companies put on a surprisingly large number of new plays every year. The most extreme example of this is the Admiral's Men, which in 1594–5 offered thirty-eight plays, including twenty-one that were new. This puts huge demands on the actors and also on the playwrights. William Shakespeare has to produce at least one new play a year and sometimes he is able to produce two, as well as acting and managing his business activities. In the amazing period 1603–6, he wrote *Othello*, *Measure for Measure*, *King Lear* and *Macbeth*. Sometimes the pressure to produce work for his company is evident, as with *The Merry Wives of Windsor* which shows signs of being hastily written. Some writers, such as Francis Beaumont and John Fletcher, collaborate on plays and together manage to produce one or two new ones every year.

The Admiral's Men

This company was originally known as Lord Howard's Men and was under the patronage of Charles Howard, 1st Earl of Nottingham and 2nd Baron Howard of Effingham. In 1585, he became Lord High Admiral and the company was renamed the Admiral's Men. The company was reorganised in 1594, with Philip Henslowe as manager and Edward Alleyn as leading actor. In 1603, they came under the patronage of Prince Henry, the elder son of King James, and were known as the Prince's Men. In 1613, after Henry's death, they came under the patronage of the Elector Palatine, husband of Princess Elizabeth. Alleyn retired from the stage in 1604 but continued as a theatre owner.

Under Queen Elizabeth, they were famous for their production of plays by Christopher Marlowe, who seems to have written some big parts including Tamburlaine and Faustus especially for Alleyn. Under King James, they have focussed on revivals together with new plays by Rowley, Dekker and Middleton. They are one of the companies that appear at court, and in 1611, as part of the Christmas festivities, they performed a play by Middleton called the *Almanak*; this was also performed at the Fortune Theatre.

The King's Men

The King's Men were known as the Lord Chamberlain's Men under Queen Elizabeth because they were under the patronage of Henry Carey, first Baron Hunsdon, who was Lord Chamberlain and head of the royal household. In 1596, he died and his son, George Carey, became the company's patron. In 1603, the company received royal patronage under King James, and was known as the King's Men. They are probably the most successful company in London. They have the benefit of being able to put on new plays written by William Shakespeare.

Until about 1600, Shakespeare concentrated on comedies and histories, but then turned to writing some of the greatest tragedies ever produced. In more recent years, he has focussed on lighter material called romances.

The company perform regularly at court and appeared there at least 107 times between 1603 and Shakespeare's death. Like the other theatre companies, they have a fantastic workload. Between early December 1605 and early January 1606 they performed the following plays at court: *Othello*, *The Merry Wives of Windsor*, *Measure for Measure*, *The Comedy of Errors* and *Love's Labour's Lost*. In the winter of 1611/12, they performed two Shakespeare plays before King James: *The Winter's Tale* and *The Tempest*, as well as *A King and No King* by Beaumont and Fletcher, *The Twins' Tragedy* by Niccols and Tourneur's *The Nobleman* and a joint production with Queen Anne's Men of *The Silver Age* and *The Rape of Lucrece*. In addition, they put on fifteen performances for other members of the royal family. The leading actor in the company is Richard Burbage, who has played the title roles in some of Shakespeare's plays, notably *Hamlet*, *Othello*, *Lear* and *Richard III* as well as parts in plays by Jonson, Webster and Beaumont and Fletcher.

Queen Anne's Men

These are also known as the Queen's Men and were the result of a merger of the Earl of Worcester's Men and the Earl of Oxford's Men. They originally performed at the Curtain in Shoreditch, but in 1607 moved to the Red Bull in Clerkenwell and tend to put on popular plays, often written by their resident playwright, Thomas Heywood, sometimes to quite rowdy audiences. Thomas Greene was the leading actor in Queen Anne's Men, having succeeded the clown Will Kemp who died in 1602. Greene got on in the world by marrying the widow of a theatrical promoter, Robert Browne, and he was famous for playing the role of an amiable ass. He is very well liked; after his death, Heywood said of him, 'there was not an Actor of his nature in his time of better ability in performance of what he undertooke; more applaudent by the Audience, of greater grace at the Court, or of more general love in the Citty'. The company sometimes appears at court: on 12 and 13 January 1612, they put on joint performances of two plays with the King's Men at the court at Greenwich, both based on the classics *The Silver Age* and *The Rape of Lucrece*.

Lady Elizabeth's Men

This company has been under the patronage of Princess Elizabeth since 1611 and consists of former child actors. It tours a lot and has a business connection with Philip Henslowe. It played the Swan where it premiered Thomas Middleton's *A Chaste Maid in Cheapside*. In 1614, it moved to the Hope and premiered Ben Jonson's *Bartholomew Fair* in the same year. The company sometimes performs at court and on Shrove Tuesday 1612 they performed *The Proud Maid's Tragedy*.

Children's Companies

The royal chapels have long had a choir which included boy singers and these gradually began to perform dramatic interludes and eventually complete plays. The fashion for boys' plays declined after 1584, but was revived by the master of the Children of the Chapel Royal, Nathaniel Giles, who took a lease of the Blackfriars Theatre and they began giving public performances from 1600 onwards.

Unfortunately, the company has been in one sort of trouble or another ever since. Giles had a legal right to compel boys to join the choir and seems to have used this oppressively. In 1601, he was in trouble in the Court of Star Chamber when a Henry Clifton accused him of kidnapping his son, Thomas, on his way to school. Giles was criticised by the court and Clifton's son was returned to him. Once King James ascended to the throne, they were given royal patronage, being known as the Children of the Queen's Revels. In 1605, they performed *Eastward Ho* by Chapman, Jonson and Marsden. Unfortunately, the play contained some anti-

Scottish jibes and in one scene Captain Seagull talked of Virginia and said he wished a hundred-thousand Scotsmen were there 'for we are all one countrymen now, ye know; and we should find ten times more comfort of them there than we do here'. Not so clever when England had just acquired a new Scottish king. The playwrights were thrown into prison and the company lost its royal title becoming Children of the Revels. In 1606, they performed *The Isle of Gulls* by John Day which satirised the Scots and the king's favourite, Robert Carr, Earl of Somerset, and portrayed a king who wasted the country's money and had corrupt advisors. There were rumours that Queen Anne went to see the play to enjoy her husband being satirised. Being rude about the king was too much and a few of the boy actors were put in the Bridewell prison for a short time and the company lost its connection to the Royal Office of the Revels and became known simply as the Children of the Blackfriars. The play remained highly controversial – the name of the publisher was removed from the printed edition and the 'king and queen' were changed to 'duke and duchess'.

In 1608, they offended the French ambassador in a play called *The Conspiracy and Tragedy of Charles Duke of Byron*, which included a scene in which the French king's wife slaps the face of his mistress. The play was taken off, but the company waited until the court was out of London in the summer and performed it again, including the offensive material. The king was furious and threatened to shut them down and some of the actors spent time in prison.

They also lost their regular playhouse as the King's Men moved into the Blackfriars Theatre in 1608 and they had to relocate to the other indoor theatre, the Whitefriars. However, their luck has changed since Philip Rosseter, lutenist to the Royal household, and Robert Keysar, a financier, took control of the company and managed to restore their reputation. They were sufficiently back in favour to be able to play at court a few times in 1611, 1612 and 1613. In the latter two years they performed *Cupid's Revenge* by Beaumont and Fletcher.

If you want to see a very different and more modern style of comedy, then the Children are the company to watch. Unlike Shakespeare's intricate romantic comedies, which were popular in the 1590s and are set in exotic locations, the Children offer plays that are more satirical, set in contemporary London and are written in words that are much closer to the ordinary speech of the people. Some of their productions, such as *Eastward Ho*, Jonson's *Epicene* and Middleton's *A Trick to Catch the Old One* are typical of this approach. Sometimes their audience is less sophisticated than they are. In 1607, their production of Beaumont's *Knight of the Burning Pestle* received a lukewarm reception because, according to the editor of the first published edition in 1613, the audience failed to recognise that this play was a parody of older plays, and took it at face value as a not very good, old-fashioned play.

Regulation

The Master of the Revels is responsible for censoring plays. The government takes the control of the theatre seriously. In 1601, Shakespeare's company nearly suffered a great catastrophe as a result of a performance of *Richard II*. The Earl of Essex was planning a rebellion and some of his supporters approached the Lord Chamberlain's Men and asked them to perform 'the play of the deposing and kyllyng of Kyng Rychard the Second on the following Saturday'. When the actors protested that it was a very old play and would only attract a small audience, the rebels agreed to pay them an extra 40s. and the curtain went up on 7 February, the day before the abortive rising. After the failure of the rebellion, Sir Gilly Meyrick, one of the leaders was accused of a number of offences, including the procurement of the performance of *Richard II*, and was executed. The players were questioned, but, perhaps surprisingly, no further action was taken against them.

Theatres in Public Houses

Under Queen Elizabeth, a number of pubs in London were used to put on plays, these included the Bell Savage on Ludgate Hill and the Bull in Bishopsgate, both of which provided outdoor performance spaces which were also used for fencing displays. The Bell and the Cross Keys, both on Gracechurch Street, were indoor venues. The Cross Keys was famous because Marroccus, the performing horse, appeared there before 1588 and the Lord Chamberlain's Men in 1594. Playing in pubs died out in the 1590s with the growth of purpose-built theatres.

Purpose-built Theatres

The outdoor theatres normally have three tiers of galleries surrounding an open space into which projects the stage. This is called the pit and is where people called 'groundlings' can stand to watch the play. Behind the stage is a 'tiring house' for changing costumes, storage and offices. There are special seating areas near the stage called Gentlemen's Rooms or Lords' Rooms. There are usually stair towers on the outside of the theatres so that people in the more expensive gallery seats do not have to walk through the yard. The back of the stage is covered by a roof called the 'heavens' and is painted with clouds and the sky. There are trapdoors in the roof and stage so that actors can make dramatic entrances.

The first two theatres in London were converted buildings, the Red Lion in Stepney, which was a former farmhouse and operated in the 1560s, and a building in Newington Butts at the Elephant and Castle, which was used from the 1570s–90s. Shakespeare probably performed there in 1593 and 1594.

The Boar's Head was originally a pub where the yard was used as a space for plays, but in 1598 it was rebuilt and in 1599 it was greatly extended. It has the advantage of being located outside the jurisdiction of the City of London as it is beyond Aldgate on the north side of Whitechapel High Street. It was home to the Earl of Derby's Men, the Earl of Worcester's Men and, since 1609, Prince Charles's Men. Other acting companies have played there as well.

Shoreditch Theatres

Shoreditch is at the north-east corner of the City of London and was the primary theatre district in London under Elizabeth.

The first purpose-built London playhouse, called the Theatre, was built there in 1576–7 by James Burbage on the site of the former precinct of Holywell Priory. A number of leading companies performed there, including the Earl of Leicester's Men, the Earl of Oxford's men and, in 1594, the Lord Chamberlain's Men, headed by James's son, Richard. In 1597, James Burbage died and his sons were unable to secure a deal with the landlord of the property, so they hired a carpenter, Peter Street, and with the actors and friends they moved the timbers to a new location on the south bank of the river in the Liberty of the Clink and reused them to build a new theatre named the Globe.

The second theatre in this area was the Curtain. It was probably built in the 1570s by a yeoman of the guard called Henry Lanman. It was used for fencing displays as well as plays.

In the prologue to *Henry V*, Shakespeare talks about the difficulties of portraying great historical events on a stage:

> But pardon, gentles all,
> The flat unraised spirits that hath dared
> On this unworthy scaffold to bring forth
> So great an object. Can this cockpit hold
> The vasty fields of France? Or may we cram
> Within this wooden O the very casques
> That did affright the air at Agincourt?

The 'wooden O' may refer to the Curtain which was probably a circular theatre. A number of Shakespeare's plays were put on there, including the premieres of *Romeo and Juliet* and *Henry V*. However, by 1611 it had fallen into disrepair.

Grenade, who visited London early in the reign of Elizabeth, remarked on the two Shoreditch theatres when walking in Moorfields, 'At one end of this meadow are two very fine theatres, one of which is magnificent in comparison with the other and has an imposing appearance on the outside.' Sadly, he was not tempted inside, preferring the bear pit on the other side of the river.

The Fortune

This was financed by Edward Alleyn and Philip Henslowe and built in 1600 in the Cripplegate area to the north of the City of London between Golding Lane and Whitecross Street. They selected this new location because their venue in Southwark, the Rose, was facing stiff competition from the newly opened and more modern Globe. The builder was Peter Street, who had also built the Globe. Unlike most of the other London theatres that are oval in shape, this one is square, but the rest of the building seems to have been consciously modelled on the Globe with three tiers of galleries and gentlemen's rooms. Curiously, the theatre in Gdansk called the Fencing School, which was built in 1611, seems to have been modelled on the Fortune. Henslowe and Alleyn moved their acting company, the Admiral's Men, there in 1600. One of its big successes was the 1611 debut of *The Roaring Girl* by Dekker and Middleton which told the story of the life of Mary Frith, better known as Moll Cutpurse, who was a fence and thief and liked to dress in men's clothes and play the lute without a licence in taverns and smoke in public. In a remarkable publicity stunt, Mary herself appeared at the end of the play, dressed in men's clothes and performed a jig and bantered with the audience. The Fortune's reputation has declined in recent years, being known for 'lewde jigges, songes and daunces' which attract 'cutt-purses and other lewde and ill disposed persons', General Sessions of the Peace for Middlesex (1612).

The Red Bull

This was built on the site of an inn in Clerkenwell in 1607 by Aaron Holland and other investors and is used for fencing as well as drama. It is one of the three large open-air theatres in London (the other two are the Globe and the Fortune). Queen Anne's Men have played at the Red Bull since 1607 and perform a range of plays including comedies and ones with domestic and London based themes. In 1612, they made the serious mistake of putting on the premier of John Webster's *The White Devil*, a dark revenge tragedy. The play was a flop. In the preface to the printed edition of the play, Webster blamed the theatre company and its audience. Put aside Webster's anger and you do get a sense of what Red Bull audiences are like. He commented on the circumstances in which the play was acted:

> in so dull a time of winter, presented in so open and black a theatre, that it wanted (that which is the only grace and setting-out of a tragedy) a full and understanding auditory; and that since that time I have noted, most of the people that come to that playhouse resemble those ignorant asses (who, visiting stationers' shops, their use is not to inquire for good books, but new books).

Theatres South of the River

Close to London Bridge is the Liberty of the Clink where there were two theatres up to 1613, the Rose and the Globe, as well as the Bear Garden. In that year, the Bear Garden was replaced by a new theatre, the Hope. Further west, in the manor of Paris Garden is the Swan. It is easy to get to the south-bank theatres by walking over the bridge, or, if that is too crowded, take a small ferry boat across – ask for Horseshoe Stairs if you want the Globe.

The Swan

In 1596, Francis Langley bought part of the manor of Paris Garden. He built the Swan Playhouse and also some houses there and in Upper Ground. The theatre was the biggest and finest playhouse in London, it has a trapdoor and a hoisting mechanism above the stage to allow special effects. It attracted such a large crowd of actors and others to the area that in October 1596 householders were ordered not to take in lodgers without permission from the constable. The playhouse was initially successful, but was badly affected when *The Isle of Dogs* was performed there. The Privy Council described it as a 'lewd plaie that was plaied in one of the plaiehowses on the Bancke Side, contanyinge very seditious and sclanderous matter' and the Swan was closed down and Ben Jonson, who had written it with Thomas Nashe, was thrown in prison with two of the actors. In 1602, the playhouse was the subject of another scandal when

Richard Vennar advertised a masque about England's triumphs over Spain entitled *England's Joy*. He announced that it would be played at the Swan on 6 November 1602, and a large audience, including many noblemen, turned up to watch it. After taking the entrance money, however, Vennar disappeared, and the audience revenged themselves by vandalising the theatre. After that it has only been used intermittently.

The Globe

The site chosen for the Globe was on some marshy gardens in Southwark near to the river. The land was poorly drained and liable to flooding so that a bank of earth had to be constructed to keep the building above the flood level. The new playhouse is larger and grander than the Theatre, the building it replaced, with the older timbers being reused as part of the new structure. Construction took several months and the new theatre was ready by 21 September 1599 when Thomas Platter made the following comments:

> After lunch about two o'clock, I and my party crossed the water, and there in the house with the thatched roof witnessed an excellent performance of the tragedy of the first Emperor Julius Caesar with a cast of some fifteen people; when the play was over they danced very marvellously and gracefully together as is their wont, two dressed as men and two as women.

At about the same time, Ben Jonson's *Every Man Out of his Humour* was also performed at the Globe. It contains a greeting to the spectators, very suitable to a new theatre. At the start of the play, after a conversation on stage, one of the characters, Asper, turns round and says, 'I had not observed this thronged round till now! Gracious and kind spectators, you are welcome.'

The new theatre was owned by the leading figures in the Lord Chamberlain's Men. The Burbage brothers, Cuthbert and Richard, owned half between them while four actors, William Shakespeare, Augustine Phillips, John Heminges and Thomas Pope, owned an eighth each.

The Globe is almost round – in fact it is a twenty-sided polygon. It is big, and the capacity is about 3,000. The thatched roof mentioned by Platter was replaced by tiles when the theatre was rebuilt following the 1613 fire.

The Rose

This was built in 1587 and is located between the Globe and the Bear Garden. It was constructed by Philip Henslowe and his then business partner John Cholmley. The acting company, the Admiral's Men which Henslowe managed, played there very successfully in the 1590s, focussing on the works of Christopher Marlowe. Edward Alleyn, the leading actor in the Admiral's Men, married Henslowe's step-daughter in 1592 and became his business partner. Originally, the Rose was a small theatre but was enlarged in 1592 to a capacity of about 2,500. It had the useful feature of a main stage and also an upper level at the back of the stage, which was ideal for Juliet's window scene in *Romeo and Juliet* or the Roman Senators looking down upon Titus in the opening scene of *Titus Andronicus*. Shakespeare's *Henry VI, Part I* was premiered there in 1592, as was Marlowe's *The Jew of Malta*, while *Titus Andronicus* was given its first performance in 1594. From 1599 the Rose began to suffer from competition from its neighbour the Globe and after the lease of the site ended in 1605, the building was abandoned.

The Hope

This was constructed in 1613 by Philip Henslowe as a dual purpose building with a moveable stage which could serve as both a playhouse and a bear-baiting venue. It was built reusing some of the materials from the bear-baiting pit on Bankside. Henslowe seems to have developed this new venture in order to take advantage of the recent fire that put the Globe out of action.

The Indoor Theatres

The two indoor theatres, sometimes called 'private' theatres, the Blackfriars and the Whitefriars, are situated in the smartest part of town.

They are capable of use throughout the year and, unlike the outdoor theatres, can play during the hours of darkness. They are much smaller than the big outdoor ones and far more expensive. While the minimum price for admission at the Globe is 1*d.*, the minimum charge at the indoor theatres is 6*d.* and so they attract a mainly better off audience, including gentlemen from the Inns of Court which are just up the road. However, not all members of their audience are wealthy, Ben Jonson talks of 'your sinful sixpenny mechanics' who sit in the oblique seats and on the seat-divisions.

Blackfriars

In 1596, James Burbage bought the freehold of the large refectory hall in the former Blackfriars Monastery. As a result of objections by local residents, he was not allowed to use it for adult actors and so he leased it to the Master of the Children of the Royal Chapel, which put on plays by boy actors. In 1608, the theatre was closed due to an outbreak of plague and the lease was handed back to James's son, Richard. He fitted the theatre out with galleries, a stage, a balcony and artificial lighting and set up a consortium comprising himself, his brother, Cuthbert, Henry Evans, William Shakespeare, John Heminges, Henry Condell and William Sly to run it and from 1609 it was used as the winter home of the King's Men, the company of which Shakespeare was a member. They would play the seven winter months in the Blackfriars and the five summer ones in the Globe. As well as Shakespeare's plays, works of other playwrights are performed here, including John Webster (*The Duchess of Malfi*) and Ben Jonson (*The Alchemist*).It is much smaller than the Globe and its audience capacity is less than a third of that of the large outdoor theatres.

Whitefriars

This is in the former library of the Whitefriars Monastery, north of the river on a lane leading from Fleet Street, and is very small, containing about 200 seats. It was set up in 1606 by Thomas Woodford and was used by companies of child actors, the Children of the King's Revels and then from 1609 to 1614 by the Children of the Queen's Revels who had moved from the Blackfriars. In 1613, Lady Elizabeth's Men used it as their winter quarters.

The Performance

Plays are advertised by playbills which are posted up. On the day of the performance, flags are flown and a trumpet sounded. Plays are usually performed six days a week and there are two or three plays on in London every day. Performance time is usually in the afternoons from 2pm until 6pm – this is because at this time business is at its quietest and people can slip away to see a show.

The admission fee is collected by people called gatherers and the charge is usually 1*d*., which entitles you to stand in the yard. An extra penny is charged for admission to the galleries and a further penny for the more exclusive seating areas, the lords' rooms or gentlemens' rooms. Thomas Platter explained:

> There are different galleries and places, however, where the seating is better and more comfortable and therefore more expensive. For whoever cares to stand below only pays one English penny, but if he wishes to sit he enters by another door and pays another penny, while if he desires to sit in the most comfortable seats, which are cushioned, where he not only sees everything well, but can also be seen, then he pays yet another English penny at another door.

The gatherers place the takings in boxes, and sometimes these are pottery receptacles like piggy banks which have to be smashed to get the money out. The gatherers then take the money to the box office where it is counted.

The costumes worn by the actors are often very fine, as Thomas Platter comments:

> The actors are most expensively and elaborately costumed; for it is the English usage for eminent lords or knights at their decease to bequeath and leave almost the best of their clothes to their serving

men, which it is unseemly for the latter to wear, so that they offer them then for sale for a small sum to the actors.

Food and drink is on sale in the theatres, as described by Thomas Platter, 'And during the performance food and drink are carried round the audience, so that for what one cares to pay one may also have refreshment.' The food includes apples, pears, dried fruit and nuts and seafood, as well as bottled beer. Members of the audience like to smoke and gamble before (and sometimes during) the shows.

The Audiences

Going to the theatre is very popular and attracts a large range of people. In the summer there are well over 20,000 seats available in theatres every week. Foreign visitors usually go to at least one play. Horatio Busino went to the theatre, but this was not too satisfactory, as he explained. He had been taken to see a tragedy 'which moved me very little, especially as I cannot understand a single word of English, though one may derive some little amusement from gazing on the sumptuous dresses of the actors and observing their gestures and the various interludes of instrumental music, dancing, singing and the like'. He also accompanied the Venetian ambassador to see a masque performed at the court at Whitehall.

The roughest members of the audience are found among the groundlings and some theatres are worse than others. An Italian, Antino Galli, said that the yard was 'an infamous place in which no good citizen or gentleman would show his face'. However, he may have been exaggerating, because in 1613, the Venetian ambassador stood among the groundlings at the Curtain Theatre.

All sorts of people can be found at theatres. Simon Forman who was an astrologer, herbalist and doctor, was a regular playgoer and wrote about his experiences in his *Book of Plays*. He described how he saw *Macbeth* at the Globe on 20 April 1610. He was, perhaps not surprisingly, very interested in the magical aspects of the play. He failed to mention the Porter's scene and he described the three witches as fairies or nymphs. He was most interested in the sleepwalking scene and, in particular how the doctor observed what was happening, 'Observe also how Macbeth's queen did rise in the night in her sleep, and walked and talked and confessed all, and the doctor noted her words.'

Forman also saw *The Winter's Tale* and *Cymbeline* at the Globe in 1611. He drew interesting lessons from the former. Regarding the character of Autolycus, he noted, 'Beware of trusting feigned beggars or fawning fellows'. In the same year, he saw a play about Richard II at the Globe, although this was not the famous play by Shakespeare, since it deals with the earlier years of Richard's reign. He was particularly interested in a fortune-telling scene, 'Remember also how the Duke of Lancaster asked a wise man whether himself should ever be king; and he told him No, but his son should be a king. When he had told him, he hanged him up for his labour, because he should not bruit it abroad or speak thereof to others.' As a fortune teller himself, Forman commented: 'Beware by this example of noblemen of their fair words, and say little to them, lest they do the like by thee for thy goodwill.'

There is a big social divide between the different sections of the audience. Thomas Dekker says that carmen and tinkers feel able to comment on plays as much as the most learned critics. For him, the solution is provided at the Blackfriars Theatre where a few gentlemen are allowed to sit on stools at the side of the stage. According to Dekker, this gives them the opportunity to make sneering comments and, most importantly, to be visible to the rest of the audience. Some playwrights have made use of these seats on the stage. In *The Knight of the Burning Pestle*, a grocer and his wife climb on to the stage and sit with the audience there and demand that the players put on a play called *The Grocer's Honour* and that their apprentice Rafe should play a leading part. In *The Isle of Gulls* by John Day, three members of the audience sitting on the stage interrupt the prologue to demand that a different kind of play be put on; one wants a satire, one a love story and one a history. Some playwrights despaired of their fashionable but inattentive audiences. In *The Magnetic Lady*, Jonson talks of 'the better and braver sort of your people. Plush and velvet outsides. That stick your house round like so many eminences – of clothes not understandings.'

In contrast, Horace Busino describes an audience that was aristocratic and took its theatre seriously, 'The best treat was to see and stare at so much nobility in such excellent array that they seemed so many princes, listening as silently and soberly as possible, and many very honourable and handsome ladies come there and very freely take their seats among the men without hesitation.'

Shakespeare and His Friends

Very little is known about Shakespeare's early life or how he became an actor and writer. He was born in 1564 in Stratford-upon-Avon, the son of a local glove maker, dealer in wool and civic dignitary. Although his father was originally prosperous, he eventually fell into debt and withdrew from public life. William married Anne Hathaway in 1582 when he was 18 and she was 26. Their first daughter, Susanna, was born six months later and their twins Judith and Hamnet were born in 1585. Hamnet's name has caused much speculation – he was almost certainly named after a local baker and friend of Shakespeare, Hamnet Sadler. Sadly, Shakespeare's son died in 1596.

What Shakespeare did next is not known – he is an actor and wears his mask when people try to find out about his life history. Some say he first trained as a butcher or that he was a schoolmaster in the country. A few claim he had to leave Stratford after a deer poaching incident. Some even think that he visited Italy – if he did, he failed to notice that the Mediterranean is not tidal or that Verona is not on the coast. In *The Two Gentlemen of Verona* Proteus rushes to catch the tide in the land-locked Verona on the non-tidal Mediterranean. Some people think it likely that he caught the acting bug when groups of players visited Stratford in 1587 – they were on tour to avoid the plague in London. What is certain is that he turned up in the capital sometime before 1592 and began working in the theatre. A few believe he started by holding the horses for people who were watching plays. Unlike Ben Jonson who attended Westminster School and Christopher Marlowe who went to Cambridge University, Shakespeare lacked an education in the Classics.

It was this lack of education and his sudden arrival on the London scene that infuriated some of his older rivals. In particular it annoyed Robert Greene, Cambridge graduate, dramatist, author of coney-catching pamphlets and a man whose main expertise was in creating his own legend. In 1592, when Greene was dying he wrote a pamphlet satirising four writers whom he does not name, with the idea that readers could work out the names of those he was criticising. One passage clearly refers to Shakespeare:

> For there is an upstart Crow, beautified with our feathers, that with his Tygers hart wrapt in a Players hyde, supposes he is as well able to bombast out a blanke verse as the best of you: and being an absolute Johannes fac totum [Jack of all trades], is in his owne conceit the onely Shake-scene in a country.

The phrase about a tiger's heart wrapped in a player's hide is a clear reference to *Henry VI, Part III* which includes the line, 'O tiger's heart wrapped in a woman's hide'. The upstart crow is probably a reference to Aesop's fable about a vain jackdaw. One day, Jupiter decided to appoint a king of the birds and instructed that they should come before him on a certain day when he would chose the most beautiful among them to be king. The jackdaw, knowing he was ugly, picked up all the most beautiful feathers of other birds that he could find and stuck them all over himself. When the great day arrived, Jupiter duly announced that the jackdaw was the most beautiful. The other birds became very angry and each one pulled from the jackdaw his own feathers, leaving the jackdaw as nothing more than a jackdaw. Some people believe that the reason for Greene's resentment was that Shakespeare's first writing job was revising the work of other writers, including Robert Greene.

By the time Greene wrote his attack, Shakespeare had probably written *The Two Gentlemen of Verona* and *The Taming of the Shrew* and was working on the Henry VI plays. By 1594 he had joined the theatrical company the Lord Chamberlain's Men and by 1599 was a shareholder. There he met a group of actors who would become his life-long friends and three of whom, John Heminges, Henry Condell and Richard Burbage, he would mention in his will. Augustine Phillips, another member of the company, left Shakespeare a 30s. gold piece when he died in 1605.

Shakespeare acted in plays as well as writing them. In 1594, Shakespeare, Richard Burbage and William Kempe the clown were paid for playing in several comedies or interludes before the queen the previous Christmas. Kempe, who had been a member of the Lord Chamberlain's Men, left the company in early 1599 and tried to make his living by clowning. In 1600, he undertook his famous nine days' wonder in which he morris-danced from London to Norwich in nine days spread over several weeks and then published a description of the event. He then travelled in Italy and on his return, re-joined another acting company, Worcester's Men. It was all too much, and by late 1603 he was dead.

In addition to Shakespeare, two of his brothers also lived in London. Edmund, the actor, and Gilbert, who worked as a haberdasher, although he seems to have moved back to Stratford where he has helped with William's business affairs.

When Shakespeare first moved to London, Shoreditch was the place where actors lived. Richard Tarleton, the famous clown, was buried in Shoreditch parish church. The Burbage family lived there, and James Burbage, the first builder of theatres, kept a tippling house there and was buried there in 1597, while in 1619 his son was also interred in Shoreditch. Christopher Marlowe lived in nearby Norton Folgate in 1589; his roommate was Thomas Watson, a poet. Marlowe got into a fight with William Bradley, son of the landlord of the Bishop Inn on Grays Inn Road, and Watson came to his aid. Watson killed Bradley and both he and Marlowe spent a time in prison, although they were ultimately released. In 1592, Marlowe was in further trouble with the constable and beadle of Holywell Street, Shoreditch. Further theatrical violence occurred in Shoreditch in 1596 when the actor Gabriel Spencer killed James Feake, the son of a goldsmith, at the house of a barber and two years later was himself killed in a duel with Ben Jonson in nearby Hoxton fields.

Shakespeare lived very close to fashionable Shoreditch, in the parish of St Helen's Bishopsgate. It is clear that he was living there in 1596 because he somehow got mixed up in a dispute between William Gardiner, a Bankside justice of the peace, William Wayte, his son-in-law, and Francis Langley, builder of the Swan theatre. The only information we have about this mysterious event comes from a single court record in which Wayte sought protection from the Court of King's Bench against Langley and Shakespeare and two women, Dorothy Soer and Ann Lee. The quarrel eventually seems to have blown over because the court took no further action. In 1597, Shakespeare's goods were valued at £5 and he was charged 5s. in taxes to the Crown. He was not very keen on paying his taxes and when the tax authorities came looking for him in 1599 he was living in Surrey in the Liberty of the Clink in Southwark, very close to the Globe.

Southwark became the popular place for actors to live at the beginning of the seventeenth century. Francis Langley owned property there, while poor William Kempe, the clown, died in the parish of St Saviour in Southwark and Lawrence Fletcher who had been comedian to King James in Scotland and subsequently joined the King's Men was buried there in 1608. Philip Henslowe, the theatrical entrepreneur, has lived in Southwark since the 1570s, while his son-in-law, Edward Alleyn, is a churchwarden at St Saviour's Southwark and has built almshouses there and supported the local grammar school.

Given the fashion for actors to live in Southwark, it is surprising that by 1604 Shakespeare had moved away to the north-west corner of the City to the parish of St Olave, where he lodged with the family of Christopher Mountjoy, a French Protestant tire maker (maker of women's ornamental headdresses) in Silver Street. Here he got involved in a curious domestic drama – the Mountjoys had a daughter called Mary and an apprentice, Stephen Belott, who was an industrious young man and stepson of one of his majesty's trumpeters. Once he had completed his apprenticeship, the Mountjoys were keen to arrange a marriage between him and Mary. Madame Mountjoy persuaded Shakespeare to act as go-between to encourage the match. He indicated to Belott that if he married Mary he would have a sum of money from Mountjoy as a dowry. However, eight years later, things had gone horribly wrong. The young married couple had moved out of the Mountjoys' house and set up their own business,

Madame Mountjoy had died and Monsieur Mountjoy had sunk into a life of dissipation. Worse, the dowry that had been promised to Belott had never been paid. Belott claimed he had been promised £60 and an inheritance of £200 in M. Mountjoy's will. Instead he had been fobbed off with £10 and some household stuff and there were rumours that Mountjoy intended to cut the Belotts off without a penny.

Stephen Belott took Mountjoy to court in 1612 and Shakespeare was called as a witness, although he was of little help to Belott. He said that Belott had been a good and industrious servant and had been well-liked by the Mountjoys. He said that he had told Belott that if he married Mary he would receive a sum of money as a dowry. But on the crucial question of what was promised to Belott, Shakespeare could not remember. In evidence he said, 'To the ffourth interrogatory this deponent sayth that the defendant promissed to geue the said complainant a porcion in marriadg[e] with Marye his daughter, but what certayne porcion he rememberethe not, nor when to be payed, nor knoweth that the defendant promissed the plaintiff twoe hundred poundes with his daughter Marye at the tyme of his decease.'

The outcome of the case was a disappointment to Belott as the court refused to make a judgement and referred the matter to the elders of the French church in London. The elders were not impressed with either party, describing them both as debauched and awarded Belott £6 13s. 4d.

By lodging in the Mountjoys' house, Shakespeare was still in close contact with the theatrical world. His friends John Heminges and Henry Condell lived in the adjoining parish and another lodger in the house was George Wilkins, who described himself as a victualler but was also a brothel keeper, pimp and writer. He collaborated with Shakespeare on *Pericles* and his own play, *The Miseries of Enforced Marriage*, was put on by the King's Men in 1606.

By 1612, Shakespeare was probably semi-retired and living in Stratford – he was described as William Shakespeare of Stratford-upon-Avon in the Belott-Mountjoy court records. However, in 1613 he made an investment in London property, buying a house in the former Blackfriars Monastery – part of the property was over a gate. He paid £80 cash plus a mortgage of £60 for the property which was probably intended as an investment, although it was very convenient for both the Blackfriars Theatre and the Globe which is just across the river. The close-knit circle of Shakespeare's friends in London can be seen from the trustees for his mortgage, which include John Heminges, the actor, and William Johnson, host of the Mermaid Tavern.

Despite his success as a writer, Shakespeare has kept up his links with his home town. His wife, Anne Hathaway, still lives there, although little is known about her, as do his two daughters – Susanna, who is married to a physician, and Judith. He has made investments in the town, buying New Place, a pretty house of brick and timber in the High Street, as well as a cottage, some grazing land and tithes which brought him in an income of £60 a year. He still owns the house in Henley Street where he was born and where his sister, Joan Hart, the only survivor of Shakespeare's seven siblings, lives. He has many friends among the locals in Stratford, including Hamnet Sadler after whom his own son was named. He is a rich man and has come a long way since his grandfather died half a century ago leaving an estate worth £38. Shakespeare announced his retirement from the theatre in Prospero's farewell speech at the end of *The Tempest*:

> Our revels now are ended. These our actors,
> As I foretold you, were all spirits and
> Are melted into air, into thin air:
> And, like the baseless fabric of this vision,
> The cloud-capp'd towers, the gorgeous palaces,
> The solemn temples, the great globe itself,
> Yea, all which it inherit, shall dissolve
> And, like this insubstantial pageant faded,
> Leave not a rack behind. We are such stuff
> As dreams are made on, and our little life
> Is rounded with a sleep.

Chapter Six

Walks

Details about precise locations and, where known, opening times of the sights mentioned can be found in Chapter 7.

Walk One – the City of London

Start at St Paul's Station, take the exit for St Paul's and walk behind the station exit and through the gates into the churchyard of **St Paul's Cathedral**. Keep right in the churchyard and follow the path round the outside of the building until you reach Paul's Cross. On this spot, Londoners would gather to hear sermons and public announcements. The fifteenth-century cross was destroyed by Puritans in the Civil War and the present one is a modern replacement.

Look to your left at the towering mass of St Paul's Cathedral. The building Shakespeare knew was burned in the Great Fire and replaced by Sir Christopher Wren's edifice. In Shakespeare's day it was possible to walk from Ludgate Hill through the cathedral to Cheapside.

Retrace your steps to New Change and proceed down **Cheapside**. This was the main east–west route across London and was its widest street. It was famous for its Eleanor Cross, its row of goldsmiths' shops and as a route for processions such as the Lord Mayor's annual parade. Walk down Cheapside until you come to St Mary-le-Bow. The building was almost totally destroyed in the Great Fire, but the crypt with its arched roof survives and is now a cafe, the Café Below. Apart from Westminster abbey and St Paul's Cathedral, St Mary was probably the most famous London church in Shakespeare's day.

Continue further down Cheapside and just at the end outside a Tesco store is a blue plaque showing that this was the location of the **Great**

Conduit, a vital source of clean water which was used by Londoners for washing and cooking.

Cross to the north of Cheapside and take Old Jewry heading north. Take the first left down St Olave's Court and cross Ironmonger Lane and enter Prudent Passage opposite. At the top of Prudent Passage, turn right on to King Street at the junction of Gresham Street (named after the founder of Gresham College and the **Royal Exchange**). The churches in this area were all destroyed in the Great Fire and the ones that remain are Wren reconstructions. There were once three churches in Gresham Street and seven more within a few hundred yards. Continue along Gresham Street crossing Aldermanbury and Wood Street on the right. The garden on the right between Staining Lane and Noble Street was the site of the Church of St John Zachary in Shakespeare's day. This was destroyed in the Great Fire and not rebuilt.

Turn right into Noble Street. Beyond St Ann and St Agnes' churchyard on the west side of Noble Street, look over the wall. You can see the remains of London's City walls which would have been much higher and surrounded the City in Shakespeare's day. Cross over Noble Street and take Oat Lane, which is part way down Noble Street. A small garden and some tombstones on your left mark the location of St Mary's Staining, another church not rebuilt after the Great Fire. At the bottom of Oat Lane take the path that goes under the modern office building (St Alban's Path), and you emerge into Wood Street and a church tower is slightly to your left. The tower on a traffic island in the middle of the street is the remains of the Wren church rebuilt after the Great Fire. St Alban's Church was on this site in Shakespeare's time. Take Love Lane on the opposite side of Wood Street and to the right of the police station. On Love Lane after the police station turn left into Aldermanbury. This leads to Aldermanbury Square, which features a bust of William Shakespeare in the centre. The Shakespeare memorial commemorates Shakespeare's friends, John Heminge and Henry Condell, who together assembled the *First Folio*, which was the first complete and accurate printed edition of Shakespeare's plays.

Leave the square by the same route you entered it, into Aldermanbury. Pass the entrance to the Guildhall Library on your left. Turn left on to Gresham Street at St Lawrence Jewry and left again into the piazza outside **Guildhall**. This has been the seat of the City of London's government since the twelfth century. The current building was constructed between 1411 and 1440. The Great Hall, the library and the medieval crypts are some of the historic rooms, which have been restored to their former glory after the fire in 1666 and bombing in 1940. The present facade dates from the eighteenth century. It is open to the public annually during London's Open House weekend in September. The library and art gallery are open to the public. The historic rooms are still used for ceremonial occasions such as the annual Lord Mayor's Banquet.

Leave the piazza in front of Guildhall. Cross Gresham Street at the lights and enter King Street. At the end of King Street turn left at Cheapside and proceed along Poultry. At the end of Poultry is a large intersection of five roads now known as The Bank. Turn right and cross Queen Victoria Street. The large building towering above you is Mansion House, this is the home and office of the Lord Mayor of the City of London and is used for civic affairs, conferences, etc. The Mansion House was not needed in Shakespeare's time because the Lord Mayors of London worked from their own houses. On the front of Mansion House is a blue plaque indicating that Stocks Market (a livestock market) was held on the site of Mansion House from 1282–1737. The foundation stone for the Mansion House was laid in 1739.

Continue round The Bank road intersection by crossing King William Street and Cornhill. On a triangular pavement and lying back behind a statute of the Duke of Wellington on a horse is the neoclassical facade of the **Royal Exchange**. The original Royal Exchange was built on this spot by Thomas Gresham, the Tudor merchant and financier. He modelled it on the bourse he had seen in Antwerp. The original Royal Exchange was similar to the current building in shape, with a central courtyard surrounded by small shops which was used for trading. The original 1571 building burnt down in the Great Fire and its successor burnt to the ground in 1838. The current building is its third incarnation.

Trading ceased on the floor in 1939 with the outbreak of war, although deals are still done in some of the cafes and restaurants that surround the courtyard.

At Bank, take Threadneedle Street and just beyond the Bank of England, fork left and go up Old Broad Street. Follow this until you come to Wormwood Street and continue until you reach Bishopsgate where you turn right. A little way down on the left is the tiny Church of St Ethelburga, the oldest medieval church in the City and one which would have been known to Shakespeare. This eastern part of the City was not touched by the Great Fire of London. Unfortunately, the church was destroyed by a bomb in 1993, although its exterior was subsequently restored to its 1411 plan. In the sixteenth century, the entrance to the church was obscured by a wooden porch and two shops. Continue down Bishopsgate on the same side as St Ethelburga's and take the next left into St Helen's Place and St Helen's churchyard.

St Helen's Church survived the Great Fire and the Blitz. Shakespeare probably worshipped here. St Helen's building dates from the thirteenth to the sixteenth centuries. It has two naves conjoined, one half being used by the parish and another by the nuns of St Helen's Nunnery. The partition between the parish church and nunnery church was removed after the dissolution of the nunnery. The pulpit is from 1615 and many of the monuments date from before the 1590s, including the effigy of Sir Thomas Gresham, surmounted with the family effigy of a grasshopper. True to form, he cleverly picked one of the few churches that survived the Great Fire and the Blitz as his burial place.

Turn left out of the church. Walk round the outside of St Helen's, along Great St Helen's. Turn right into St Mary Axe. On the corner of St Mary Axe with Leadenhall Street is the Church of St Andrew Undershaft. Turn left into Leadenhall Street for the entrance. Built between 1520 and 1535, it survived the Great Fire and the Blitz. It has a memorial to John Stow, the author of the 1598 *Survey of London* (died 1605) to the left of the sanctuary. The statue of Stow holds a quill pen in his hand. Once every three years the Lord Mayor oversees the ceremonial replacement of the quill pen (due in early April 2017). The undershaft referred to was the large maypole which was set up annually in the spring until the early sixteenth century.

From St Andrew's continue left down Leadenhall Street. At the next junction on the left with Creechurch is St Katherine Cree. The tower is early Tudor (built 1509). In the church, Sir Nicholas Throckmorton is buried (died 1571). The rest of the building is late Jacobean.

Continue along Leadenhall Street until the junction with Aldgate and Fenchurch Street. That large stone block with a pitched roof on the top of it, on the curb where Fenchurch Street meets Leadenhall Street, is the Aldgate Pump. A pump has stood near this spot since before Stow's time (possibly from 1535), although in Tudor times it was situated slightly further east. The current pump is Victorian. It was recognised as the spot marking the start of the East End and is reputed to be the place where the last wolf was shot in London which is recorded by the plaque with a wolf's head on it. From Aldgate Pump, turn back up Aldgate heading past St Botolph without Aldgate. Continue to Aldgate Tube station.

Walk Two – Southwark

Start at St Paul's Station. Take exit 2 from the station which leads to St Paul's Cathedral, Old Bailey and Newgate Street. Turn right out of the station exit. Stay on the pavement and at the traffic lights turn right into New Change. Proceed down New Change. Keep St Paul's Cathedral and the railings of the churchyard to your right. Cross Cannon Street at the traffic lights. Turn right along Cannon Street (it becomes Carter Lane) keeping St Paul's Cathedral on the opposite side of the road to your right. Take the second left into the street that is called Peter's Hill on the left-hand side of the road and Sermon Lane on the right. Carry on straight ahead down the steps crossing Knightrider Street. You should see the Millennium Bridge ahead of you. Carry on straight across Queen Victoria Street at the traffic lights.

Walk on to the Millennium Bridge. Pause half way across the bridge. Look back to the north bank of the river. To the left of the bridge is the modern building of the City of London School for Boys. The school's foundation has its roots in the fifteenth century bequest of John Carpenter, the town clerk of London in the reign of Henry V and one of the founders of the Guildhall library. Look about you as you stand in the centre of the bridge. In the sixteenth century, the river would have been bustling with small craft very much like the Grand Canal in Venice today. On this part of the river scores of ferrymen would be rowing groups of customers across or up and down the river. The ferries plied upstream taking passengers to Lambeth Palace, Richmond, Hampton Court and beyond and downstream to the Pool of London and The Tower, Limehouse, Deptford and Greenwich. Commercial boats delivering beer barrels and produce and rich people's comfortably upholstered and covered private barges mingled with the wherry water taxis. Looking towards Southwark on the south bank, to your right along the bank would have been the bear pit, a tall circular building, much like the theatres of the day, with a flag flying if they were running an event that day. To your left along Bankside, huddled together, the many brothels, or stews as they were called, and numerous taverns with the theatres towering over them

Continue your walk across the bridge. Turn east along Bankside, which has been a thoroughfare since the thirteenth century. When you get to the **Globe Theatre** go down the steps and walk to the buildings to the right of the Globe museum. Between the houses, which are of a later date, is a tiny blocked off alleyway with its name plate declaring it is Cardinal's Cap Alley. In the late 1590s and early 1600s the alley led to a tavern called the Cardinal's Hat. It was popular with people from the theatre. Edward Alleyn dined there in 1617 and John Taylor, the poet, later ate there with some players.

Retrace your steps a few metres so you are in front of the Globe Theatre with its thatched roof and its whitewashed lath and plaster body. The original Globe Theatre was situated 274m south east of the current Globe. It was slightly smaller than the building you see today. The current Globe was built in 1997 following the design of a sixteenth-century theatre; it offers a very authentic reproduction of the Shakespearean theatre experience. You can stand in the pit to watch a Shakespeare play at a matinee during the summer months, although it is pricier than the 1*d*. it cost in Shakespeare's time. Or you can sit on a bench under cover for rather more money. The museum is open to the public and theatre tours are available or you could book to see a play and taste the full experience.

Within the Globe complex is a smaller theatre, called the Sam Wanamaker Playhouse. This is a replica of an early Jacobean theatre, like the **Blackfriars** across the river, and is lit by candles for the productions.

Keeping New Globe Walk to your right, continue east along Bankside. At the corner of Bankside and Bear Gardens turn right into Bear Gardens. Soon after turning into Bear Gardens on the left, in the wall by the Real Greek restaurant, is the last surviving example of a ferryman's seat. The seat would originally have been much closer to the river bank, next to the stairs down to the river where the ferries were moored.

Half way down Bear Gardens just before the junction with Park Street, is the site of Davies Bear Gardens, one of the well-known **bear gardens** of Elizabethan Southwark. Turn left out of Bear Gardens into Park Street; 56 Park Street, beyond the Globe Education Centre on your left, is the site of the **Rose Theatre**. It was the first of the purpose-built theatres to be constructed in Southwark. It was not as large or as popular as the Globe or the Swan theatres which were built nearby and in 1605 its lease ran out, it closed and was probably demolished in 1606.

Walk 46m further on. Immediately after walking under Southwark Bridge on the left is the Financial Times Building. The north-west corner of the building is thought to be the site of the Elephant Tavern, mentioned in *Twelfth Night*. The remains of the original Globe Theatre were found in 1989 at 123 Park Street on the south side of the street. The outline of part of the walls and layout is marked out on the paving in the small open area that backs on to Anchor Terrace.

Bankside was the entertainment area of Elizabethan and Jacobean London and offered all kinds of leisure activities including drinking establishments, stews, playhouses and bear baiting. Many taverns lined Bankside in Shakespeare's time. The Anchor, at 34 Park Street, is sometimes said to be the only one that remains, but although there was a pub there in earlier times, by Shakespeare's day it had become houses.

After The Anchor pub, Bankside turns right. Follow it and take the next left under the bridge into Clink Street. This is an original, narrow street from Shakespeare's time and is named after the infamous gaol that was located there. Immediately in front of you to the right, where the road narrows, is the Clink Gaol Museum. This is now a tourist attraction, but in Shakespeare's time there was a gaol nearby in the basement of Winchester Palace, the palace of the Bishop of Winchester, just to the east of this building. By the sixteenth century, the gaol was used for religious prisoners who did not follow the teachings of the Church of England. The current tourist attraction is based in a nineteenth-century warehouse building. The Clink was so feared that its name has become slang for prison.

Half way down Clink Street (after the junction with Stoney Street) to the right is a fourteenth-century gabled wall containing a huge skeletal rose window, and another wall and some foundations which are remnants of the Bishop of Winchester's palace, an imposing building that stood here from the twelfth to the eighteenth centuries. The Diocese of Winchester was much larger than today, covering much of the south-eastern corner of England and extending up to the Thames at Southwark, where the bishop owned lands. Bishops in medieval times needed residences in London to maintain contact with the monarch.

Follow the road round into Cathedral Street. In St Mary Overy's Dock is moored a replica of Sir Francis Drake's ship, the *Golden Hind*, which circumnavigated the world in 1577–80. In Shakespeare's lifetime the original *Golden Hind* was a tourist attraction. It was beached in Deptford but eventually the ravages of weather and souvenir hunters meant that the wooden ship completely disintegrated. The replica can now be visited for Tudor fun days, battle experiences or an overnight stay 'with Tudor style dinner and continental breakfast'.

Turn left following Cathedral Street. At a small junction take the right fork. Southwark cathedral can be accessed through the gate in the railings on the left. This thirteenth-century church became a cathedral only in 1905 but was a large parish church in Shakespeare's time, dedicated to **St Saviour**. It has numerous connections with Shakespeare. Shakespeare paid for the funeral and burial of his actor brother, Edmund, in the church in 1607. There is a ledger stone to mark Edmund's death aged 27. In the cathedral there is also an alabaster monument to Shakespeare (installed in 1912) and above it a stained glass window depicting many of his famous characters (unveiled 1954). Many of the actors of the King's Men Company which Shakespeare had belonged to lived in the parish and probably worshiped in St Saviour's Church every Sunday.

When you have seen the cathedral, turn left and continue across the churchyard. Climb the steps to London Bridge. At the top of the steps turn right, away from the river. You are now in Borough High Street which was historically the main thoroughfare to London from the south. It led directly to **Old London Bridge**. Everyone travelling on foot or by horse would have to cross London Bridge to get into London. What a bottle-neck it was! Carts carrying vegetables, cattle and sheep coming to the London markets from Kent farms would have to wait their turn here among the travellers and Londoners who couldn't afford the few pence ferry fare. The bridge was narrow, being only 12ft wide, and shops and houses lined either side, resembling the Ponte Vecchio in Florence. The crowds pushed their way along the bridge going in both directions. A gate at the southern end closed at night and opened again in the morning. By 1600 there were approximately 200 shops and buildings on the bridge including the church and a public latrine.

Cross Borough High Street to the east side of the street and walk south past the entrance to London Bridge main line station. Follow the traffic away from London Bridge and under a criss-cross of railway bridges over the road. Cross St Thomas Street and continue south along Borough High Street. Off to the left at regular intervals are lanes or yards bearing the names of taverns and inns that formerly lined the approach to London Bridge. So you will see King's Head Yard, White Hart Yard, George Inn Yard, Talbot Yard, Queen's Head Yard as you walk down Borough High Street.

At 63 Borough High Street, a plaque set up by the Historic Southwark Society marks the place where the White Hart Tavern stood. This was the tavern that Shakespeare names as the rebel Jack Cade's headquarters in *Henry VI, Part II*. Continue walking south along Borough High Street until you reach the George Inn. The present building dates from 1677, but there was a George Inn on the site in Shakespeare's time. It is an authentic example of a galleried seventeenth-century inn. Only the south side of the inn survives, the rest having been demolished to build railway warehouses in the nineteenth century.

Continue walking down Borough High Street. Between Newcomen Street and Mermaid Way stood the notorious Marshalsea prison. In the sixteenth century it housed prisoners of all types. Ben Jonson was incarcerated there in 1597 because he was the joint author of the play *The Isle of Dogs*, which was describe to the Privy Council as a 'lewd plaie that was plaied in one of the plaie houses on the Bancke Side, contaynynge very seditious and sclandrous matter'. Chistopher Brooke, a poet, was jailed there in 1601 for helping his friend, the poet John Donne, marry a 17-year-old girl, Ann More, against her father's wishes. The Marshalsea was moved to a new site further down Borough High Street in 1811 and the perimeter wall can be seen just beyond the library. The tiny garden in Tabard Street was the graveyard for the debtor prisoners.

Walk back up Borough High Street on the left (west) side. Turn left at Union Street and walk up towards Redcross Way. On the north (right-hand) side of Union Street just before you reach Redcross Way is **Crossbones Graveyard**. This was an unconsecrated burial ground for prostitutes and their children in Shakespeare's time and later a graveyard for paupers. In recent years a local group have cared for the graveyard and made it very attractive. Turn right into Redcross Way and follow the side of the Crossbones site on your right.

Turn right into Southwark Street. At the junction with Borough High Street cross Southwark Street to the north side of the street. As you walk north up Borough High Street towards the river, Stoney Street and Bedale Street, to your left, lead to Borough Market, which might be worth a detour. In Shakespeare's time this was a general market for meat, seasonal fruit and bread. Nowadays Borough Market is known as a speciality food and vegetable market open most days of the week and very popular. Now the market is covered but in the sixteenth and seventeenth centuries, the stalls were open to the elements.

After crossing Bedale Street to your left and going under the railway bridges, walk north towards the river. Cross the road after you have gone under the railway bridges just before passing Southwark cathedral on your left.

Cross London Bridge. To your right, looking downstream, is the Pool of London, the area from London Bridge to Limehouse. The Thames is deep and tidal at this point. In the late sixteenth century the bridge barred the way to large sailing vessels so the Pool of London was the furthest upstream that the main sea-going ships could dock. It was lined with wharves where goods were brought in from overseas and stored or transferred to barrows or carts to take them to market. In the morning the wharves at Billingsgate would have been teeming with porters unloading scores of fishing boats bringing in their catch for sale at Billingsgate fish market on the waterside. The Pool of London would have been particularly busy at high tide when the largest vessels could sail up the Thames as far as London.

Once you have crossed London Bridge, turn right into Monument Street and right again into Fish Street Hill. At the bottom of Fish Street Hill is Lower Thames Street. Cross Lower Thames Street at the traffic lights to its south side and enter the Church of St Magnus Martyr, slightly to your right.

St Magnus Martyr was on the north-east end of Old London Bridge. As you came over Old London Bridge into the City, the church would have been to your right at the clearing called St Magnus Corner. Like the bridge approach on the south side, this was a place where crowds gathered and jostled with seasoned travellers and Londoners crossing to Southwark to visit the playhouse, the taverns, bear baiting or a night out with a prostitute. Empty farmers' carts pulled by horses waited to get on to the bridge with milk-maids' empty pails dangling from the yokes across their shoulders and peasants pushing market barrows trudging back to the villages of Bermondsey and Rotherhithe. This corner was the place where, in Tudor times, the mayor could order public proclamations to be pronounced, with the knowledge there would be a large audience.

The medieval church was burnt down in the Great Fire, which started a stone's throw away, and was rebuilt by Wren. The portico arch under

St Magnus's tower formed the pedestrian entrance to Old London Bridge when it was enlarged in 1763. By that time the shops and houses on the bridge had been demolished and an additional pedestrian lane added, in a vain attempt to prevent traffic jams building up at the crossing. The Church of St Magnus the Martyr still has links to the Old London Bridge. There are still two stones from the Old London Bridge to see a few metres beyond the church's portico in the churchyard, while embedded in the archway of the tower (to your right as you pass through the arch) is a wooden strut, part of the Roman wharf found across the road in Fish Street Hill in 1931. This discovery demonstrates how the Thames was much wider in medieval and Roman times. A model of Old London Bridge from about 1450 can be viewed inside the church (to the left of the west entrance). Cross back over Lower Thames Street and walk north back up Fish Street Hill (away from the River). When you reach the large intersection of roads at the top of the hill to your right is **Eastcheap**, sometimes called Great Eastcheap. In Shakespeare's time there were a number of famous taverns in this street, none of which remain.

To your left is Cannon Street and in front of you is Gracechurch Street. Turn left into Cannon Street and continue along to Cannon Street Station, opposite which on the north side of the street is **The London Stone**, an irregular piece of limestone standing about 0.5m high. It is secured in the wall of a shop, currently (2016) a branch of WH Smith. This stone was considerably larger and more imposing in Tudor times and until 1962 it was left open to the elements. Souvenir hunters have taken their toll and now it is enclosed behind an iron grille, making it barely visible from outside the shop. Go into the shop and look behind the shelves by the door for a good view of the stone enclosed in its glass case. It was a very famous London landmark in Shakespeare's lifetime on the south side of the street, then known as Candlewick Street. It represented the heart of London, the place where oaths were sworn, debts redeemed and contracts agreed. The stone is wreathed in myth and tradition. It may have been placed nearby in Roman times as the point in Londinium from which distances were calculated. According to folklore, London is safe as long as the stone is safe. It was certainly in Candlewick Street in 1188 when there is a written reference to Henry Fitz-Ailwin de Londenstane, the first Lord Mayor of London. Jack Cade, in the 1450 uprising against King Henry VI, is recorded to have struck the stone when he entered the City of London. Shakespeare dramatised the event in *Henry VI, Part II*. Jack Cade strikes the stone with his staff and says of himself: 'Now is Mortimer lord of this city. And here, sitting upon London-stone, I charge and command that, of the city's cost, the pissing-conduit run nothing but claret wine this first year of our reign. And now henceforward it shall be treason for any that calls me other than Lord Mortimer.'

Continue west along Cannon Street. At the Mansion House station junction where Queen Victoria Street crosses Cannon Street, cross Queen Victoria Street on the north side (on the opposite side from the underground station entrance). A few yards along the west side of Queen Victoria Street on the left is a narrow street called Watling Street. Watling Street was one of the main thoroughfares of Shakespeare's London. It traces its origins back to the Roman period. It has probably not increased in width since the sixteenth century and gives you an idea of the claustrophobic warren that was the maze of streets that made up Shakespeare's City of London. You may catch a glimpse of St Paul's Cathedral at the end of Watling Street.

From Watling Street turn first right into Bow Lane. Investigate the court on the left, Groveland Court with Williamson's Tavern at the end. The old City was made up of many shady, dead-end courts like Groveland Court where there were shops, dwellings and taverns crammed together. Return to Bow Lane and off on the right is another lane, Well Court, which, if you follow it through leads into Queen Street.

Return back through Well Court to Bow Lane and turn left into St Mary-le-Bow churchyard. With St Mary-le-Bow Church to your right and the statue of Captain John Smith behind you, turn left out of St Mary's churchyard into Cheapside. At the end of Cheapside you will see St Paul's Cathedral towering above you. Cross New Change towards the cathedral. The station entrance is to your left as you walk north towards Newgate Street.

Walk Three – Legal London

Start at Chancery Lane Station, taking the exit for Fetter Lane. You emerge from the station on a road called High Holborn. The name derives from its position on high ground above the deep valley that the River Fleet flows through just east of here. 'Hol' refers to the hollow that the river flows through and bourne is an archaic word for river. Hence Holborn. In fact, on maps of the time the river is referred to at this point as the Holborn.

The legal area of London where the Inns of Court and Inns of Chancery were located is on the western edge or just outside the old City of London. This location arose from a decree of Henry III in 1234, which dictated that no institution training lawyers should be found in the City of London, so they gravitated to the western side of the City nearest Westminster and the courts. The Inner and Middle Temple were liberties of the City of London, they were within its borders, but not subject to its jurisdiction. Lincoln's Inn and Gray's Inn are located outside the old City boundary. All four of these major Inns of Court grew up in the late fifteenth century and were and still are enclosed within their own walls.

Turn east. You will see an Elizabethan building jutting out over the pavement. This is the front of **Staple Inn**. The entrance to Staple Inn has shops on the ground floor and typically Tudor half-timbered upper floors leaning out above the pavement. This terrace is all that remains of the medieval Staple Inn. It was set up in the late fourteenth century and was an enclosed collection of buildings arranged round courtyards making up one of the Inns of Chancery. Staple Inn, like the other Inns of Chancery, was a less important Inn than the four main Inns of Court. Each Inn of Chancery was connected with one of the major Inns of Court, in Staple Inn's case it was attached to Gray's Inn. Inns of Chancery like Staple Inn were institutions where trainee lawyers were educated and lived. Once they had a basic training, they would be promoted to the main Inn, to continue their studies. All the Inns of Court and Inns of Chancery were similar to the Oxford and Cambridge universities at the time with trainees and professionals living and eating together within a walled community.

In the centre of the row of shops is an arch with a passageway leading to the rest of Staple Inn. Walk through into the peaceful and secluded courtyard. Unfortunately, Staple Inn was badly bombed in the Second World War and the buildings on the site are reconstructions. The hall in the courtyard opposite the gateway is a faithful copy of the 1580s Staple Inn hall destroyed in the Blitz.

Return through the archway to High Holborn. Turn right to continue your way east. Cross Furnival Street and Dyer's Buildings. After a number of shops on the right there is a narrow court entrance at 23 Holborn with Barnard's Inn etched into the stone above. Barnard's Inn was another Inn of Chancery attached to Gray's Inn. Walk down through the alleyway, which is only open on weekdays. You pass through several courtyards until you come to the final courtyard. Here to the left as you enter the courtyard is the location of Gresham College, founded by the will of Sir Thomas Gresham. The hall, which is only open to the public when Gresham lectures are held, is a late fifteenth-century building with sixteenth-century embellishments, such as the linen fold panelling and a restored roof that includes the only crown posts in Greater London. The room directly below the hall has some chalk and tile walling dating from the Roman era. Turn right and approach the busy junction of seven roads that is called Holborn Circus. Cross at the traffic lights to the north side of Holborn (by the time you reach here, the road that was called High Holborn has become Holborn). Then cross Hatton Garden so you are now at the start of Charterhouse Street.

Almost immediately there is a gated road to the left which is **Ely Place**. This was the location of Ely Palace, the London residence of the Bishop of Ely from the early fourteenth century until 1576. It was a lavish palace with 58 acres of extensive gardens, vineyards, ploughed lands and orchards, known particularly for its saffron and strawberries. The palace at Ely Place finds a place in at least two Shakespeare plays. In *Richard III* when the Duke of Gloucester wants to get rid of the Bishop of Ely, he says: 'My Lord of Ely, when I was last in Holborn/ I saw good strawberries in your garden there./I do beseech you send for some of them.' John of Gaunt spent his last seventeen years living in Ely Place after his home at the Savoy was looted and burnt down by Wat Tyler's men during the Peasants' Revolt of 1381. It is at Ely Place that Shakespeare gives Gaunt his famous 'Scept'red isle' speech. All that remains of the Bishop's Palace is the Church of St Etheldreda. The church stands at 14 Ely Place set back from the rest of the buildings. It was the chapel of the palace and dates back to 1290 in the reign of Edward I. When Sir Christopher Hatton leased the property from Elizabeth I, he let the crypt out as a tavern so that services were sometimes interrupted by drunken outcries. Ironically, the church has returned to the old faith and the crypt is once again let out as a restaurant. From St Etheldreda's Church retrace your steps and find the narrow alleyway, Ely Court. Half way along is Ye Olde Mitre Tavern, which traces its history back to 1546. The tavern, although old, is not the original building. Until the 1980s there was a cherry tree in the tavern's garden which, it is claimed, was danced round by Elizabeth I and Sir Christopher Hatton. Now the trunk of the dead tree is preserved in a glass case to the right of the main entrance to the bar. Continue to walk through the alley. Turn left into Hatton Garden, named after Sir Christopher Hatton, who lived here. The road is now known as the centre of the London jewellery, gold and diamond trade. Walk to the end of Hatton Garden where it meets Holborn. Turn right and walk back along Holborn toward Staple Inn on the other side of the road, crossing Leather Lane.

As you pass a large red building at 138–42 Holborn (approximately 20m from Hatton Garden), you will see a blue plaque recording the site of Furnival's Inn which was demolished in 1897. This was another one of the Inns of Chancery, like Staple Inn and Baynard's Inn across the road. Furnival's Inn was attached to Lincoln's Inn. Continue along Holborn past Brooke Street and Gray's Inn Road until you reach the public house called The Cittie of Yorke. Despite its appearance, this pub is not ancient, but dates from the 1920s, although some writers claim there have been pubs on the site for 500 years. Just before The Cittie of Yorke is an alleyway on your right. Turn into this alleyway and proceed through the entrance into **Gray's Inn**, the short name of The Honourable Society of Gray's Inn. Walk through a second archway under the buildings into South Square.

This is now the smallest of the four Inns of Court but in its heyday, in the time of Queen Elizabeth I, it was the largest. It still resides on the same site within the same walls but many of the old buildings disappeared under the rubble of the Blitz. One building that mostly survived was the hall. In the sixteenth century the great hall (on the north side of the square) would have been the central focus of life in the Inn because the students who lived within the walls were compelled to eat dinner and supper there. Unfortunately, Gray's Inn's Hall is now not normally open to the public, other than for tours. It has stained glass, paintings and shields that have survived from the Elizabethan period. The huge carved wooden screen at the entrance to the hall is traditionally thought to have been donated by Elizabeth I, the patron lady of the Inn, and to be carved from wood from a captured Spanish galleon after the Armada of 1588.

The *Gesta Grayorum*, an account of the revels performed at Gray's Inn in 1594, records that *The Comedy of Errors* was performed at the Hall on 28 December 'by a company of base and common fellows' as part of the law students' Christmas revels.

In the centre of South Square stands a statue of Sir Francis Bacon, one of the famous Elizabethans who were members of Gray's Inn at the height of its powers. He was long associated with the Inn. He was admitted in 1576 and called to the Bar in 1582. Later he became the first Bencher and was elected Treasurer of the Inn. Walk through the archway to the north west of South Square. As you go through the archway note the names listed on either side of the staircases at 10 South Square, recording the individual barristers and tenants residing or practising on that staircase. This is the norm in all the Inns of Court. Turn left and walk under the next archway. To the right are the gardens of Gray's Inn, or Walks as they are called. They were originally laid out by Sir Francis Bacon in 1606. It is thought that the remains of the ancient catalpa tree, crushed by another tree in the hurricane of 1987 and located on the west side of the Great Walk, may have been planted by Sir Francis Bacon. More plausibly it could have been imported from the East and planted a century later. The Walks are still a calm haven for quiet contemplation away from the hurly-burly of London streets. After a turn round the Walks depart through the same gate. Take the smaller gate straight ahead of you out of the Inn precincts into Fulwood Place. Walk the whole length of Fulwood Place and emerge into High Holborn.

Cross High Holborn at the traffic lights and turn into Chancery Lane which is the road that leads south almost opposite Fulwood Place. Part of the way down Chancery Lane, you come to a large red-brick building with a very large Tudor arch enclosing a stout double wooden gate. This is the gateway to the Honourable Society of **Lincoln's Inn**. The gatehouse was built in 1518–21. The three coats of arms above the gate are those of Sir Thomas Lovell, Henry VII and the Earl of Lincoln. Sir Thomas Lovell was the Treasurer or the Head of the Inn at the time of the construction. It was restored in 1695, as evidenced by the date stone above the architrave. The great oak gates were in place in the sixteenth century. The whole of the site occupied by the Inn was acquired in 1580 but the east side of the site where New Square stands was undeveloped in Shakespeare's day. In the 1580, the Inn consisted of the gatehouse, some chambers and a chapel. Before you enter the Inn look at the brick walls which were built in 1562 to separate the Inn from the people in the street. It is reported that Ben Jonson, when a young man, helped with the brickwork. Walk in through the small gate to the right of the main gate into the Inn.

Walk north (turning right away from Old Buildings) along Old Square. At the end of Old Square is the chapel. The open undercroft that you can walk through has fifteenth-century fan vaulting and a bricked-in archway, which were in place in 1600. The chapel itself was rebuilt in the first decades of the seventeenth century. The poet John Donne was admitted to Lincoln's Inn in 1592 and practised as a lawyer after his marriage to Anne More left him hard up. Later, he took holy orders in the Anglican Church and acted as preacher at Lincoln's Inn.

Much of the tradition of the Inns had already been fixed by the late sixteenth century, other than the uniform for the barristers and judges. All English barristers still belong to one of these Inns of Court. In Shakespeare's time barristers lived and practised out of chambers in the Inns of Court and the Inns supervised the training of barristers and their apprentices. Nowadays, the chambers, or partnerships of barristers working together, may be located beyond the walls of the Inns. Lincoln's Inn, like the other Inns, had and still has its own great hall, chapel, chambers and gardens. It is enclosed, like the other Inns, to keep the professionals distinct and segregated from the surrounding area.

Walk through the undercroft of the chapel to New Square. Beyond this point the Inn buildings are of later date. Walk straight across the north end of New Square with the gardens to your left to the Victorian Gatehouse, at the back of Lincoln's Inn.

Walk through the Victorian gateway with two turrets. Enter the large square with the park in the centre which is Lincoln's Inn Fields. Until the English Civil war, this area was, as its name suggests, open fields. In 1683, it was the scene of the public beheading of Lord William Russell, son of the 1st Duke of Bedford, for his involvement in the Rye House Plot. The executioner inexpertly required four cuts to complete the job and it is said that Lord William turned to the executioner and said, 'You dog, did I give you 10 guineas to use me so inhumanely?' Walk along the outside of Lincoln's Inn Fields, keeping the gardens to your right and passing the large red-brick building to your left which has Patent Office written on it. At the corner of Lincoln's Inn Fields where the road becomes Sardinia Street there is a road to the left called Portsmouth Street. Turn left into Portsmouth Street.

On the left is The Old Curiosity Shop at 13–14 Portsmouth Street, London, WC2A 2ES. This quaint shop dates from the sixteenth century. It survived the Great Fire of 1666 and has the typical overhanging upper storey and great wooden beams of a sixteenth-century building. In the past it has been a dairy and an antique shop. Currently, it sells smart shoes. The building is claimed to have inspired Charles Dickens to write the book of the same name.

Cross Portugal Street and slightly to the right enter Clements Lane, which leads into Grange Court which you cross to get into an alley down the side of the law courts called Clement's Inn. This Inn was one of the minor Inns of Chancery, but nothing remains of it other than its name and a plaque. To the left of Clement's Inn now are the Royal Courts of Justice which face on to The Strand. The Royal Courts of Justice in

Shakespeare's time were located at the Palace of Westminster. The Inns were ideally placed between the City of London and the law courts in Westminster, a mile or so down The Strand and Whitehall.

Look east (left) along Fleet Street. This is one of the main roads in the City of London. It began at the bridge over the River Fleet just outside the old City walls at what is now Ludgate Circus. Near the junction of Fleet Street and Chancery Lane is a standing stone in the middle of the road. This is the original location of Temple Bar. The area from Ludgate to Temple Bar was under the jurisdiction of the Corporation of London and a gate was erected here to restrict entry to the City. The Temple Bar gate survived the Great Fire but was enlarged by Wren and subsequently removed in 1874 to ease the traffic flow and pedestrian access along Fleet Street. Its site is marked by a memorial in the middle of the street which includes a pedestal with reliefs of Queen Victoria and the Prince of Wales and is surmounted by a griffin.

Close by is 17 Fleet Street which survived the Great Fire of London of 1666 and is the only remaining building in Fleet Street from the time Shakespeare lived in London. It was built in 1610 as a tavern called The Prince's Arms. Later it changed its name to The Fountain and was visited by Pepys. In the late eighteenth century it became the home of a museum, Mrs Samuel's Waxworks. The whole building was moved slightly south when Fleet Street was widened in 1905. On the first floor is a wonderful Jacobean room with wood panelling and intricate plaster ceiling known as Prince Henry's Room, although it is not known whether there were any connections with Prince Henry, James I's eldest son. It is not currently open to the public.

An archway was inserted in 17 Fleet Street in the eighteenth century. It is an entrance to the Honourable Society of the Inner Temple (known as the **Inner Temple**). Enter the Inner Temple through this gateway. The Inner Temple and the Middle Temple are separate associations of lawyers which are located next to one another in an area of London called The Temple. The Temple gets its name from the church built by the Knights Templar, the twelfth-century military crusaders, in this locality. The Order of Knights Templar was abolished in 1312 and 150 years later lawyers moved into the area. The church still stands and remains the oldest part of the Inner Temple, as most of the early buildings there were destroyed in the Great Fire or the Blitz. Once through the pathway the Temple Church is visible to your left. The church is a Royal Peculiar, which answers to the monarch rather than to any bishop. It is not part of any diocese. The Round Church was built in 1185 and the Chancel followed in 1240. It is famous for its nine stone effigies of knights. South of the church is the Inner Temple Hall. Skirt Inner Temple Hall on the west side. On the south side of the hall is Crown Office Row. The entrance to the Inner Temple's lovely garden is through a gate opposite Crown Office Row.

The garden covers 3 acres and is normally open to the public between 12.30 and 3pm on week days. In the late sixteenth and early seventeenth centuries the garden was well known to Londoners. Shakespeare dramatically places the start of the Wars of the Roses in this beautiful garden. In Shakespeare's lifetime, the Inns of Court were regarded as finishing schools for young aristocrats who had no intention of practising law. So in *Henry VI, Part I*, Shakespeare imagines the young aristocrats of the Yorkist and Lancastrian factions ejected for being rowdy in Inner Temple Hall and spilling out into the Inner Temple garden where Richard Plantagenet, later Duke of York, says, 'From off this briar pluck a white rose with me.' The Duke of Somerset responds, 'Pluck a red rose from off this thorn with me.' And the other aristocrats one by one pick either a white or a red rose.

After a walk round the Inner Temple garden exit through the same gate. Turn left out of the gate and along Crown Office Row. Leave the Inner Temple by the gate and cross Middle Temple Lane. The building on your left is **Middle Temple Hall**. Turn right and enter Middle Temple by Fountain Court. Many buildings on both sides of Middle Temple Street belong to the Honourable Society of the Middle Temple. The Middle Temple flourished in the sixteenth century. It had particular connections with the West Country at that time. Sir Martin Frobisher, Sir John Hawkins and the founder of the Jamestown Settlement of 1607, Bartholomew Gosnold, were all members of the Inn. It is said that Sir Francis Drake had some connection with the Middle Temple. He was not admitted but dined there several times. Tradition has it that the cupboard on which young barristers sign the register when they are called to the Bar at Middle Temple was made from a hatch cover of the *Golden Hind* (perhaps some member of Middle Temple took a rather large souvenir after it was opened to tourists when it was finally beached at Deptford).

The Middle Temple Hall survives more or less as it was when it was built in 1562–73, a wonderful example of an Elizabethan hall. It has an amazing double hammer beam roof, built out of oak from Windsor forest. The hall's carved wooden screen was installed in 1574. It has extensive wooden panelling decorated with coats of arms. The 29ft-long high table was reputedly donated by Queen Elizabeth I. It was made from three logs from a single great oak tree grown in Windsor forest. The trunk was floated down the Thames for the table to be constructed *in situ*. There is original Elizabethan stained glass including one pane with Elizabeth I's royal insignia. The minstrels' gallery was used by John Dowland among others. It was the location for the first performance of Shakespeare's *Twelfth Night* on Candlemas, 2 February 1602 to mark the end of the Christmas Revels.

Retrace your steps across Middle Temple Lane through the gate into the Inner Temple by Crown Office Row. At the junction with Mitre Court, Tudor Street is almost straight ahead. Follow Tudor Street to the end where it meets New Bridge Street. Turn right and at 14 New Bridge Street is an archway which is all that remains of Bridewell (see pp. 79–80), once a royal palace turned house of correction. Much of the prison that stood here in 1600 was destroyed in the Great Fire of London, 1666.

Cross New Bridge Street. Turn right and walk along to The Black Friar public house. This is on the site of the **Blackfriars Theatre** where Burbage and Shakespeare performed.

As you travel down New Bridge Street you are walking on the mouth of the Fleet River as it flows into the Thames. From Ludgate Circus look north up Farringdon Street. From here in 1600 you would have seen a busy river inlet with boats moored on either side at thriving wharves. The

Fleet River now runs in a sewer under your feet. Until the mid-eighteenth century it was an open river flowing through a deep valley which ran down what is now Farringdon Street straight ahead of you beyond Ludgate Circus. Pause a moment before you cross New Bridge Street. You are standing where the bridge stood linking the gate in the City walls, called Ludgate, with Fleet Street, the route to Westminster.

Cross New Bridge Street and cross Ludgate Hill so you are on the north-east side of Ludgate Hill. Walk up Ludgate Hill and take the second left into Old Bailey. Walk to the end of Old Bailey and turn right into Newgate Street. A few yards from the corner with Old Bailey you will see a blue plaque on the Old Bailey courts building explaining that Newgate was on this spot until demolished in 1777. Newgate was not only a gate in the City walls but the gatehouse building was a notorious prison. Ben Jonson, playwright and poet, was imprisoned in Newgate on 22 September 1598 for killing his fellow actor Gabriel Spenser in a duel. He was freed next day by pleading benefit of clergy. Another well-known Londoner of the early Jacobean period imprisoned in Newgate was Mary Frith, alias Moll Cutpurse, the notorious pickpocket, fence and cross dresser.

Continue up Newgate Street to St Paul's Station.

Chapter Seven

Surviving Buildings from Shakespeare's Time

L ondon has undergone huge change since Shakespeare's day. Even during his lifetime, the City changed rapidly and the dissolution of the monasteries, colleges and hospitals led to major redevelopments with monastic property either being converted to other uses or demolished to make way for housing. Parish churches that had previously shared a building with a local community of monks or nuns were redesigned and in some cases partially demolished. The aristocracy was leaving the old City to move nearer to the court and building fine houses along The Strand.

Fifty years after Shakespeare's death, London suffered its greatest catastrophe when the Great Fire which started in a baker's shop in Pudding Lane spread throughout most of the City. Virtually everything was destroyed except for some properties in the north-east corner near St Bartholomew's Hospital. The destruction was terrible and almost complete – most of the buildings which Shakespeare would have known, St Paul's Cathedral, St Mary-le-Bow, the Royal Exchange and the taverns where he met his friends all went. The Southwark theatres survived the fire, but the Globe was demolished in the 1640s, while the Hope seems to have lasted until the 1680s as a bear-baiting arena.

A few churches survived, including St Helen's Bishopsgate where Shakespeare may have worshipped, but this was badly damaged by bombs in 1992 and 1993 and has been restored, while the nearby St Andrew Undershaft, another survivor, lost its medieval stained glass because of the 1992 bomb. The oldest church in London, St Ethelburga's in Bishopsgate, also survived the Great Fire, but was destroyed by an IRA bomb in 1993 and has been rebuilt.

What has survived, pretty much, is the medieval street pattern. You can walk down streets the location and layout of which must have been familiar to Shakespeare. There have been a few significant changes. You can no longer walk though St Paul's Cathedral from Ludgate Hill to Cheapside. The rebuilding of London Bridge in 1831, 30m upstream from its ancient location, and the associated development of King William Street was a major change in the street pattern, as was the building of Queen Victoria Street in 1861.

The following list describes those surviving buildings that Shakespeare might have seen as well as some reconstructions and memorials. Some are not usually open to the public, but it is worth checking out London Open House day for special events.

Chelsea

Crosby Hall

Crosby Hall was built in 1461 in Bishopsgate, in the City of London. Richard III lived here when he was Duke of Gloucester. Shakespeare was familiar with the place and in his play *Richard III* he sets the plot to kill Richard, Duke of Gloucester there. The building was owned by Sir Thomas More. In 1908 it was dismantled and the materials stored to be used on a new site in Chelsea, where it was re-erected in the 1920s, coincidently on land once owned by Sir Thomas More. It has since been extended in a Tudor style. Not open to the public, Danvers Street, Chelsea, Greater London SW3 5AZ.

Chelsea Old Church

The church was thirteenth century with two private chapels, one built in 1528 for Sir Thomas More while the other belonged to the lord of the manor. The church was bombed in the Second World War and has been restored; the More Chapel was the least badly damaged. It has a number of Tudor memorials. Queen Elizabeth may have worshipped here before she became queen, as did Lady Jane Grey. Usually open on Tuesday, Wednesday and Thursday from 2pm to 4pm, corner of Old Church Street and The Embankment SW3 5DQ.

West End

St James's Park and Palace

Henry VIII acquired the Hospital of St James for Lepers and built a small palace to escape from court life at Whitehall. The park, which is the oldest royal park in London, was also acquired by Henry and was developed by James I, who kept exotic animals there. Palace not open to the public, SW1A.

Westminster Abbey

See pp. 81–2. Open daily, but times may vary, SW1P 3PA.

Jewel Tower

Built around 1365 to house Edward III's treasures as part of the medieval palace of Westminster, it was known as the 'King's Privy Wardrobe'. It has an exhibition covering all three floors of the tower which details the Jewel Tower's history and changing role and includes a model of the lost Palace of Westminster. Open daily, March to end of October, open on Saturday and Sunday in winter months, Abingdon Street, opposite Houses of Parliament SW1P 3JX.

Westminster Hall

See pp. 18 and 82. Pre-booked tours available, London SW1A 0AA.

Charing Cross

Replica of Eleanor Cross

See pp. 78–9, outside Charing Cross Station is a replica of the Eleanor Cross that once stood near this site. The original cross was slightly to the east of the replica at the junction of The Strand and Whitehall and was destroyed on the orders of Parliament in 1647. It was much higher than the replica, standing about 125ft, whereas the current version is 70ft.

Aldgate

Aldgate Pump
See p. 137. Junction of Aldgate High Street, Fenchurch Street and Leadenhall Street.

St Katherine Cree
See pp. 83–4, 137, 86 Leadenhall Street EC3A 3BP.

Bank

The Royal Exchange
See pp. 40–3, 135–6. Stores open 10am to 6pm, bars open 8am to 11pm, Bank EC3V 3LR.

Barbican

The Barbican contains a number of fragments of the City Walls which would have been seen by Shakespeare.

Ironmonger's Hall
This is a 1920s vision of what a Tudor house would have looked like. The Ironmongers Company's medieval hall was located in Farringdon and a Tudor building was constructed on that site in 1587; this survived the Great Fire. It was rebuilt in 1745 and damaged by a bomb in 1917. After the First World War, it was demolished and a new mock-Tudor building opened in Aldersgate. Not usually open to the public, Shaftesbury Place, Barbican EC2Y 8AA.

St Giles Without Cripplegate
This church survived the fire because, as its name suggests, it was outside the walls of London. It was the church where Edward, the infant son of Shakespeare's brother Edmund, was buried in 1607. The building was badly damaged by the Cripplegate fire of 1897 and by bombs in 1940. It was rebuilt after the war on the basis of the original plans of the 1545

building, but some parts of the medieval church are visible. Usually open 11am to 4pm, Monday to Friday, Fore Street, Barbican EC2Y 8DA.

St Alphage's

This garden on London Wall is all that remains of the former Priory Church of St Alphage and includes a section of London Wall. Off London Wall EC2Y 5EL.

Barber-Surgeons Garden

This is a modern garden but is very close to the location of the Tudor garden maintained by the Company of Barber Surgeons in Monkswell Square and contains specimens of herbs used in medicine and surgery. Their hall, which was nearby, was used for anatomy demonstrations. Monkwell Square, Wood Street EC2 5BL.

Bishopsgate

Leadenhall Market

The market building is Victorian, but the market dates back to the fourteenth century. EC3V 1LT.

St Helen's Church

See pp. 83, 136, Great St Helen's, London EC3A 6AT.

St Ethelburga's Church

See p. 136, 78 Bishopsgate EC2N 4AG.

St Andrew Undershaft

See p. 136, for access, contact St Helen's Church, 0207 283 2231, St Mary Axe EC3A 8EP.

London Bridge and Blackfriars

See pp. 59–67, open daily, Lower Thames Street, EC3R 6DN.

St Andrew by the Wardrobe

The church that Shakespeare would have known on this site was burned in the Great Fire and its replacement by Wren was severely damaged in the Second World War. The church had a genuine connection with Shakespeare because his company played at the nearby Blackfriars Theatre in the winter and he bought a house in Ireland Yard, also nearby. There are memorials to Shakespeare and the lutenist John Dowland in the church. Open Monday to Friday, 8.15am to 4.15pm, St Andrew's Hill, London EC4V 5DE.

Holborn

Staple Inn

See pp. 146–7, hall not usually open to the public, High Holborn, London WC1V 7QJ.

Barnard's Inn

See p. 147, hall is accessible for public lectures, Holborn EC1N 2HH.

The Old Curiosity Shop

See p. 151, 13 Portsmouth Street WC2A 2ES.

St Etheldreda's Church, Ely Place

See p. 148, open daily, closed Sunday afternoon, 14 Ely Place EC1N 6RY.

Ye Olde Mitre

See p. 148, open Monday to Friday, 11am to 11pm, 1 Ely Place EC1N 6SJ.

Gray's Inn

See pp. 148–9, the grounds are open to the public, 12pm to 2pm on weekdays, but the hall is not usually open, 8 South Square WC1R 5ET.

Chancery Lane

Temple Bar
See p. 152.

Lincoln's Inn
See pp. 150–1, the grounds are open to the public, but not the buildings, WC2A 3TL.

Fleet Street

Prince Henry's Room
See p. 152, not currently open to the public, 17 Fleet Street.

Temple Church
See pp. 152–3, open to the public, weekdays 10am to 4pm, closed Saturdays and only open for services on Sunday, but hours may vary, Temple EC4Y 7BB.

Middle Temple Hall
See p. 154, only open for pre-booked tours of ten or more people, Middle Temple Lane, London EC4Y 9AT.

Cheapside

St Mary-le-Bow
See pp. 47–8, open Monday to Friday, also Café Below in the Crypt, St Mary-le-Bow Church, Cheapside EC2V 6AU.

Memorial to John Heminge and Henry Condell
See p. 134, Aldermanbury Square.

Guildhall
See pp. 80, 135, open during Open House weekend. Library and art gallery open Monday to Saturday 10am to 5pm and Sunday 12pm to 4pm, Gresham Street EC2V 7HH.

Cannon Street

London Stone
See pp. 144–5, can be seen from the street or inside WH Smith, open Monday to Saturday, 111 Cannon Street EC4N 5AR.

Clerkenwell

The Clerk's Well
The well that gave the area its name can still be seen in Farringdon. Apparently the site of medieval plays performed by the parish clerks of London, the well can be seen at Well Court, 14–16 Farringdon Lane EC1R 3AU. On the subject of underground water, the River Fleet can be heard nearby under a drain cover in Ray Street opposite The Coach and Horses pub, but watch out for traffic. EC1R 3DJ.

Saint Bartholomew the Great
See pp. 84–5, open to the public. Giltspur Street EC1A 7BE.

Cloth Fair
This street was where cloth was sold during Bartholomew Fair. The house at 41 and 42 Cloth Fair was built between 1597 and 1614 and is the oldest house in London, having been saved from the Great Fire because it was within the walls of the priory. Scheduled for demolition in the 1920s, it managed to survive and has been restored. Not open to the public.

Charterhouse
See pp. 80–1. This was originally a Carthusian monastery which was converted by Lord North into a Tudor mansion. The buildings range from the fourteenth century onwards and include Tudor and Jacobean structures. A fourteenth-century gatehouse can be seen from Charterhouse Square. Pre-booked guided tours, conducted by one of the brothers, are available. Sutton's Hospital, Charterhouse Square EC1M 6AN.

St John's Gatehouse

Built in 1504, but heavily restored in the nineteenth century, this was the grand entrance to the priory of the Order of St John. William Hogarth's father once set up an unsuccessful Latin speaking coffee shop here. Across from the gate is the priory church with a fine Norman crypt, housing an alabaster effigy of a Castilian knight (1575) and a battered monument to the last prior. The structure now houses the museum of the Order of St John of Jerusalem. St John's Gate, St John Street EC1M 4DA.

The Hand and Shears

This pub is nineteenth century, but there has been an alehouse on this site since the Middle Ages. Bartholomew Fair was traditionally opened from the steps of the alehouse by the Lord Mayor. It was used by the Merchant Taylors to check the fabrics sold at the fair and as a place to settle disputes between customers and merchants. 1 Middle Street EC1A 7JA.

Tower of London

See pp. 67–77. William I's fortress, Tudor prison, former home of the Royal Mint and the Royal Armouries and current home to Beefeaters and ravens, the Tower is open daily. EC3N 4AB.

Southwark

Cardinal's Cap Alley

See p. 138. Not open to the public. SE1 9DT.

Shakespeare's Globe

See pp. 121–2. Tours available and museum. SE1 9DT.

Shakespeare's Globe, Original Site

See p. 139. Park Street; the postcode for Anchor Terrace is SE1 9HQ.

Bishop of Winchester's Palace and Clink Prison

See p. 140. Clink Prison, 1 Clink Street SE1 9DG.

Golden Hind
See pp. 88, 140. 1 Pickfords Wharf, Clink Street SE1 9DG.

Ferryman's Seat
See p. 139. Set into the wall of the Real Greek Restaurant, Bear Gardens, Bankside SE1 9HA.

Rose Theatre
See p. 122. 56 Park Street, Bankside SE1 9AR.

Borough Market
See p. 142. Southwark Street, London SE1 1TL.

Southwark Cathedral, Formerly St Saviour's
See pp. 130, 140–1. Open daily, London Bridge SE1 9DA.

White Hart Yard
See p. 141. White Hart Yard, off Borough High Street, London SE1 1NX.

The George Inn
See p. 142. 75–7 Borough High Street SE1 1NH.

Crossbones Graveyard
See p. 142. Opening details for the garden are available online at http://www.crossbones.org.uk/, junction of Redcross Way and Union Street, Southwark SE1 1TA.

Lambeth

Lambeth Palace
The London residence of the Archbishop of Canterbury. Set on the south bank of the Thames, it includes some buildings such as the chapel, the Lollards Tower and the early Tudor brick gatehouse which could have been seen by Shakespeare. Organised tours are available, SE1 7JU.

Canonbury

Canonbury

The manor house of Canonbury was built by William Bolton, Prior of St Bartholomew's. On the dissolution it was handed over to Thomas Cromwell and in the 1590s it was rebuilt, including the tower by Sir John Spencer, Lord Mayor of London. Sir Francis Bacon, the scientist and philosopher, lived there for a time. It was recently used as a Masonic research centre. Canonbury Tower, Canonbury Place N1 2NQ; not open to the public.

Deptford

St Nicholas's Churchyard

Christopher Marlowe was killed in Deptford in 1593 in a brawl as a result of an argument over the bill at a tavern run by Eleanor Bull. Details of his death were not known to scholars until 1925 when Leslie Hotson the Shakespearean scholar found the coroner's inquest into his death. This showed that Marlowe had argued with Ingram Frizer, grabbed his knife and wounded him. Frizer had retaliated and knifed Marlowe who died. The coroner's verdict was self-defence and Frizer was pardoned. Marlowe was buried in an unmarked grave in the churchyard. There is a memorial plaque on the wall. Deptford Green SE8 3D.

Greenwich

Queen Elizabeth's Oak Tree

The remains of an oak tree in Greenwich Park, planted in the twelfth century, it was a huge oak by the sixteenth century and it is said that Henry VIII danced with Anne Boleyn in its shade and that Queen Elizabeth used to enjoy refreshments under its boughs. Greenwich Park SE10 8XJ.

Hampton Court

Hampton Court Palace

See pp. 90–2. As well as the Tudor buildings, you can see the baroque palace built by King William and Queen Mary in the late seventeenth century. Open daily, East Molesey, Surrey KT8 9AU.

Homerton

Sutton House

The red-brick Tudor house is an amazing survival in the middle of Hackney. Built in 1535 by Sir Ralph Sadleir, a courtier and administrator under Henry VIII. Originally known as 'the bryk place', it has undergone many adventures in its long life, including being occupied by squatters, but is now in the hands of the National Trust. Open Wednesday to Sunday, 2 and 4 Homerton High Street, Hackney E9 6JQ.

Hoxton

The Geffrye Museum

Set in eighteenth-century almshouses, the Geffrye Museum includes a replica of a 1630 room from a house in Aldersgate which has long been demolished. The room is a facsimile of the hall of the house, the main living room and it is lined with replica oak wainscot panelling. Open Tuesday to Sunday, 10am to 5pm, Bank Holiday Mondays 10am to 5pm, 136 Kingsland Road, London E2 8EA.

Barking

Eastbury Manor

Set incongruously in the middle of a Barking housing estate and close to the Lodge Avenue flyover, Eastbury Manor is a rare example of a genuine Tudor building in the London area. Built by Clement Sysley, a London merchant during the reign of Queen Elizabeth, it was allowed to decay over the years, but has been recently restored. There are tenuous but unlikely links to the Gunpowder Plot and it is believed to be haunted. Open Wednesday, Thursday and Sunday, Eastbury Square, Barking IG11 9SN.

Bermondsey

Edward III's Manor House

The foundations of a manor house built by Edward III are still visible near the river in Rotherhithe. The building used to be surrounded by water on three sides so Edward could approach it by boat. The reason for its construction is not known, but historians have assumed that it was built to allow Edward to enjoy falconry, flying birds of prey across the low-lying marches. Later monarchs were not such keen falconers and by Shakespeare's day it was in private hands. Bermondsey Wall E, London SE16 4NB.

St Mary Magdalen, Bermondsey

The church belonged to Bermondsey abbey until the dissolution. It was largely rebuilt in the seventeenth century, but the lower portion of the tower is late medieval. 193 Bermondsey Street SE1 3UW.

Bexley

Hall Place

A magnificent Tudor house built in 1537 for Sir John Champneys, a wealthy merchant and former Lord Mayor of London. The walls, which are made of flint and rubble, have a distinctive Tudor checkerboard pattern. Open daily, Bourne Road, Bexley, Kent DA5 1PQ.

Eltham

Eltham Palace

The palace is based on a moated bishop's palace from the fourteenth century. It was heavily used as a royal palace until the sixteenth century. It was one of the small number of palaces that could accommodate the entire court of 800 people. Edward IV built the surviving great hall. Henry VIII spent much of his boyhood there, but with the rebuilding of Greenwich and Hampton Court, both of which were more modern and accessible by river, Eltham fell out of use, and it became a farm and parts were demolished. In the 1930s it was acquired by the millionaires Stephen and Virginia Courtauld who built a modern house incorporating much of the surviving medieval structures. They used it to display their collection of art and to entertain the rich and famous of their day. During the war it was taken over by the army and is now managed by English Heritage which is restoring it to its 1930s glory. Opening times vary, Court Yard, Eltham, Greenwich SE9 5QE.

Richmond

Richmond Palace

See p. 90. The palace was demolished in the Commonwealth period and all that survives is part of the gatehouse which is now a private house on Richmond Green. Not open to the public.

Woolwich

Charlton House

The house, which is a fine example of Jacobean architecture, was built by Sir Adam Newton, tutor to King James I's elder son, Prince Henry. It is owned by the local council and run by a trust and is available for weddings and other events. The library is open to the public, as are the gardens and tours and events are arranged, Charlton House, Charlton Road SE7 8RE.

Further Reading

Barron, Caroline, Christopher Coleman and Claire Gobbi, 'The London Journal of Alessandro Magno, 1562', *London Journal* (1983)

Bowsher, Julian, *Shakespeare's London Theatreland*, 2012

Bridge, Sir Frederick, *The Old Cryes of London*, 1921

Fisher, F.J., 'The Development of London as a Centre of Conspicuous Consumption in the Sixteenth and Seventeenth Centuries', *Transactions of the Royal Historical Society* (1948)

Forsyth, Hazel, *The Cheapside Hoard: London's Lost Jewels*, 2013

Grenade, L., *The Singularities of London, 1578*, London Topographical Society Publication 175, 2014

Hentzner, Paul, *Travels in England During the Reign of Queen Elizabeth*, 1894

Jones, Nigel, *Tower: An Epic History of the Tower of London*, 2011

Mason, Dorothy E., *Music in Elizabethan England*, Folger Shakespeare Library, 1958

Morley, Henry, *Memoirs of Bartholomew Fair*, 1859

Ordish, Thomas Fairman, *Shakespeare's London*, 1904

Pierce, Patricia, *Old London Bridge: The Story of the Oldest Inhabited Bridge in Europe*, 2001

Porter, Stephen, *Shakespeare's London: Everyday Life in London, 1580–1616*, 2009

Razzell, Peter (ed.), *The Journals of Two Travellers in Elizabethan and Early Stuart England, Thomas Platter and Horatio Busino*, 1995

Saunders, Ann, *The Royal Exchange*, London Topographical Society, Publication 152, 1997

Saunders, Ann, *St Paul's: The Story of the Cathedral*, 2001

Sim, Alison, *Food and Feast in Tudor England*, 1997

Sim, Alison, *Pleasures and Pastimes in Tudor England*, 2009

Stone, Lawrence, *Family and Fortune: Studies in Aristocratic Finance in the Sixteenth and Seventeenth Centuries*, 1973

Stow, John, *A Survey of London Written in the Year 1598*, 2009

Index